Anjum's New Indian

Anjum's New Indian

Photographs by Vanessa Courtier

QUADRILLE

To Adarsh,
for believing in me
more than I do myself.

This edition first published in 2009 by
Quadrille Publishing Limited
Alhambra House
27–31 Charing Cross Road
London WC2H 0LS

Text © 2008 Anjum Anand
Photographs © 2008 Vanessa Courtier
Design and layout © 2008 Quadrille
Publishing Ltd

Editorial director Anne Furniss
Creative director Helen Lewis
Project editor Gillian Haslam
Designer Lucy Gowans
Photographer Vanessa Courtier
Food and props styling Susie Theodorou
Make-up artist and hair stylist
  Grace Anhua Ma
Map Sarah McMenemy
Production director Vincent Smith
Production controller Marina Asenjo

Cataloguing in Publication Data:
a catalogue record for this book is
available from the British Library.

ISBN 978 184400 789 9

Printed and bound in China

Contents

Introduction

Where does one start when writing about the regional foods of India – a country with a population larger than that of most continents and equally diverse?

There is, in fact, no such thing as 'Indian cuisine'. The story of the food is a complex one, a saga that has to take into account the regional, religious, historical and geographical influences over the last millennium. One would need to drift back to the beginning to understand how travellers from foreign lands have merged with the local people and produce, to create the cuisine of the different regions, each with their very own style, identity and taste.

We all have preconceptions as to the food from different nations and these are often influenced by how they are represented in our own countries. But the reality is often quite different. Most of our experiences of Indian food have been restaurant-led, but the early Indian restaurants developed a hybrid cuisine to please the British palate with only a cursory nod to the authentic. This was deliberate. The British might love a curry today, but to unleash the full might of spices on uninitiated palates would probably have been bad for business. However, over time, people acquired the taste for the food and the offerings have become more authentic and more regional.

Many of us do still perceive Indian food as tasting of a generic 'curry', so eating proper Indian food is often a revelation. Dishes are often lighter than expected, with a lot of importance placed on freshness, aroma and colour. Indians are immensely proud of their food and take time to cook it every day for their loved ones. We consider it the healthiest food to eat.

Depending on the region, dishes might be spicy or light, a touch sweet or a little tart. They are always well balanced and nutritious. Some regional food is rustic, but other regional specialities are the outcome of centuries of perfecting the cooking in the kitchens of the Maharajas. The regions have their own food

customs and mores. Some will start a meal with poppadoms, while others will eat them at the end to cleanse their palates. Some dip their snacks in chutney; others mark the change in flavours and eat it in between the main course and dessert. It is a cuisine you can spend your life getting to know, and it is there to be discovered by all those who are interested.

India's food has been heavily influenced by three main external groups over the last thousand years. Of these, the Moguls, who came from Central Asia, were perhaps the most important. They brought with them their love of red meat, rice, nuts and their own exotic fruit, and even today many of their dishes, such as biryanis, kormas and pilaffs, are household names. The Portuguese colonized Goa for 450 years and, aside from completely changing Goan food to incorporate their eating habits, they also introduced India to one of her most precious ingredients, the chilli. The British left their culinary footprint in India with a hybrid cuisine and a variety of new eating habits. The most obvious, but sometimes least known, gift to India was tea. It is typical of the Indian, however, to take something foreign and make it their own by adding spices to it, in this case creating the famous masala tea.

Even with these external influences, most people ate the seasonal food that grew on their doorstep. This was dictated by the land and climate. I am always surprised by the variety of ingredients that grow there. In the winter months, you can buy fresh strawberries on the roads of Kolkata and find oranges from Darjeeling. Apples, pears, grapes and berries come from the northern state of Kashmir. Sole, trout, whitebait, mackerel, sardines, crab and lobster are all found in her waters. You can eat fantastic meals of partridge, venison, quail, pigeon, duck and beef in the different regions. Coastal food will contain coconut and curry leaves. Northern food will have an abundance of dairy produce. There are many types of oil and even more varieties of grain that are widely eaten. All of these fantastic ingredients make the food so individual and exciting.

With all these differences, there is, however, one common thread that runs through the cooking of the regions – the use of spices. It is said that, thousands of years ago, ancient sages understood the inherent healthy properties of spices and, to ensure the people consumed a daily dose of nature's own supplements, interwove them into the very fabric of the food. Spices are still the hallmark of Indian food and to get the real flavours of the regions, you have to become familiar with them. There is no blended 'curry' powder; each spice is used independently to add flavour to an ingredient. Each region takes from the huge spectrum of spices and uses them in different proportions and in their own ways to create their own distinct tastes. So, aside from a chicken curry, one might choose one solitary defining flavour for a dish, so chicken might be cooked predominantly with cumin, coriander or cardamom, garam masala or dried pomegranate seeds.

Our culinary relationship with India may be hundreds of years old, but I find it has developed into an honest one only over the last decade or so. This book is only a snapshot of the breadth and depth of cooking of this subcontinent. It is impossible to explore every regional influence and include all the best dishes. Some of the dishes have been included for their simplicity, others for their history and some for their relevance to a region; needless to say, I believe them all to be full of flavour and pleasure. This book has been a culinary journey for me as much as it might be for you, and I hope you enjoy it as much as I have.

Anjum

Before You Start

I know that many people will want to move straight to the recipe section of this book, but please take a moment to read these notes. I have been cooking long enough to know that when it comes to a new cuisine, even professionals can make assumptions that will lead to an inauthentic dish. It is worth having a quick read to ensure your dish turns out as it should.

Tomatoes

Tomatoes come in all shapes, sizes and colours. In India, we use tomatoes for both their sweet and sour tastes, so when a tomato is cooked down it becomes a little sweet but is also a little sour. In some of the modern varieties of tomato, this sour element seems to be missing and the tomatoes are now primarily fresh and sweet. Using these would definitely change the entire character and balance of an Indian dish, with too much sweetness and not enough tartness.

The best tomatoes to use in Indian food are the cheap cooking tomatoes, rather than plum, cherry or vine-ripened ones. But tomatoes are nature's bounty and will not always be exactly as you want them to be, so you should always try a dish before serving and adjust with a squeeze of lemon juice or a pinch of sugar, if necessary.

Chillies

Chillies, so synonymous with Indian food, were actually brought to India by the Portuguese in the sixteenth century. They were seafarers and picked up ingredients on their travels – the chilli is originally from South America. Before the chilli, Indians used black pepper and a spice called long pepper to add heat to their food, but this was harder to grow and more susceptible to damage from certain insects. The chilli was soon adopted and now India is the largest producer and probably consumer of the chilli.

There are so many different types of chillies, from the round, bulb-like ones used in Gujarati food to the long, thin green ones used in Punjab and the large, mild red ones found in Kashmir and Goa. The type of chilli you use does make a difference to the dish, both in flavour and heat. It is probably best to stock up on a packet of mild dried red chillies and buy the thin, finger-like green ones as and when you need them.

Red chilli powder has different levels of heat depending on the provenance and variety of chilli that has been ground, and also whether the seeds and membranes have been removed before grinding as they are the hottest part of the chilli. Unfortunately, there is no way of telling how hot one packet is from the next. I look for a deep colour. I often buy a packet of red chilli powder called degi mirch, which has a wonderful deep red colour but not much heat. I use it for colour, but you can also add a little paprika for extra colour without the heat.

Meat

In the West, chefs cook with stocks, whereas in India they cook with bones.

I usually buy my lamb from an Asian butcher. It is generally leg meat and he cuts it into large cubes with the bone left in. The logic of keeping the bone is that a chef will not want to waste any flavours and a lot of the 'meaty' flavour is in the bone. In India, many professional cooks add extra bones to their dishes for additional flavour, removing them before serving. It does take longer to cook meat on the bone, but it also ensures that the lamb or chicken does not dry out so quickly and is really tender. The meat usually cooks with the masala, so it ends up taking the same amount of time.

You can use lamb that is boneless, and I have done so in recipes where there are other ingredients in the same dish and I don't think anybody wants to

start picking out the bones. Use whichever is easiest and available, but do remember that if you use boneless cubes of meat, the masala has to be well cooked before adding the meat and you will need to adjust the cooking times accordingly. Lamb can take less than 10 minutes if boneless and from the rump, or it can take 45 minutes over a slow heat if from an older lamb with the bone in. You can generally tell from the texture and softness, but if in doubt, cut one piece open and check it is done how you like it.

Fish

When cooking fish in a gravy, it is best to cut the fish into large steaks. This will help to hold the fish together and stop it from flaking easily, and the bones will add flavour to the dish at the same time. I know that most people hate picking bones out of their fish so, if that is the case, do use fillets. Just choose a fish with firm flesh and do not stir the pan once it is inside, just shake to amalgamate the ingredients.

When buying fish, try to buy from a fishmonger as they have lots of experience and will tell you which fish is fresh and which will be good for a gravied dish. And, if asked nicely, they will scale and clean the fish, cut or fillet it as necessary.

Lentils

Unless otherwise stated in the recipe, a lentil curry should be cooked to the point where the lentils are soft and indistinct from the water but have not turned to mush.

Indians use a wooden whisk called a ghunti to help. It is placed straight into the pot of lentils and when you rub the handle between your palms, it whisks the soft lentils around it into a purée while leaving the others whole. This thickens the dish to the right consistency. If you don't have one, you can always use a normal whisk to help.

Skinning Nuts

The skins of nuts have no flavour and are considered difficult to digest. And in the case of pistachios, they obscure the beautiful green nugget hidden inside. I do make the effort to skin nuts before using them, regardless of the cuisine, as it makes a difference to the dish. The easiest way of doing this is to place them in a bowl and pour over boiling water. Once the water has cooled, the skins will slip off easily when rubbed. If you are preparing a large quantity, place them all in a clean, dry tea towel and rub. The coarse texture of the towel will help to remove the skins, especially those of pistachios.

Browning Onions and Masala

In the West, cooks normally only brown the meat. In India we brown our onions and masala (see page 251) and sometimes our meat, but even then this is often done in the gravy so both are browned together. We call this technique bhuno, and it can apply to anything.

The onions are the easy bit. I cook onions over a low–medium heat until they are soft, then turn up the heat to colour them. Colouring too quickly might lead to a brown onion that has not yet been properly cooked through. The deeper their colour, the more flavour, but obviously don't go too close to a dark brown – a deep golden colour is fine.

I also often 'brown' my masala. This step adds an extra depth of flavour to the dish and deepens the flavours of the tomatoes and onions; when there is a meat included, it is even better. This just requires you to 'cook' the masala over a medium–high heat and stir often as it reduces into a thick rich paste, then add water from a boiling kettle for the gravy.

Basic Recipes

Black Masala

This masala blend is from the state of Maharashtra. I recently experienced it at the house of a friend who cooked a dish with such an unusual, unfamiliar taste. I soon discovered and fell in love with black masala, also known as Goda masala. It is a blend of roasted spices and coconut, ground together into a powder. It is sweeter and milder than garam masala, although some versions can be quite peppery. I like the blend when it is harmonious enough to go in anything, and then I add extra chilli or pepper if I am in the mood. You can't find all the traditional ingredients for this masala outside India so I have left a couple out, but it is still absolutely delicious. It does require a little patience to dry roast the spices, but once you have spent the 15 minutes or so it takes from start to finish, you will just love the resulting sweet, aromatic blend.

30g unsweetened desiccated coconut
2 tbsp sesame seeds
50g coriander seeds
1½ tsp vegetable oil
1 tsp black peppercorns
1 star anise, broken up
2 tbsp cumin seeds
1 tsp caraway seeds
8 cloves
2 black cardamom pods
1 large dried red chilli
½ stick cinnamon
2 bay leaves

Heat a large frying pan and dry-fry the coconut until it has become quite golden but before it turns truly dark. Scrape immediately into a bowl. Add the sesame seeds to the pan and stir-fry until golden, then add to the coconut. Add the coriander seeds to the pan and stir-fry, over a moderate heat, until well browned but not dark brown. Add to the coconut.

Add the oil to the pan and fry the remaining ingredients together, stirring, over a low heat until they become aromatic and the cumin seeds have changed colour. Add to the bowl and leave to cool.

Grind the mixture to a fine powder in a spice blender, then store in a sterilized, airtight container for up to 3 months.

My Garam Masala

This is the quintessential spice blend. Garam means hot, but here it refers not to spice but to the heat it generates in the body. There are so many spice blends in India, and as a Punjabi, I would say garam masala is from the Punjab. However, there is also a garam masala in Bengal, but this comprises only three sweet spices so bears little resemblance to this mix. It is used in Kashmir too, so I concede that garam masala might not be Punjabi, but they do use an awful lot of it in both powdered and whole form. In Punjab, every house has its own version, and this is my family recipe. It is spicy and fragrant. If you have mace, add in two blades, and if you want to temper the spiciness add 2 teaspoons of coriander seeds to the mix. If you do make this version, use less than the amount stated in any recipe as it will be stronger. Add to taste.

4 small dried bay leaves
7 black cardamom pods
¾–1 tsp black peppercorns
2 tsp cumin seeds
5g piece of cinnamon or cassia bark
5 cloves

Grind everything together to a fine powder and store in a sterilized jar in a dark, cool place for maximum freshness. It will last for months and months.

Goan Red Spice Paste

This is a spicy, vinegary paste from the beautiful region of Goa. It is great with meat, chicken and fish; I have used it in a few recipes to get you started. Just remember when you cook with it, it is all raw so it does need to be well cooked before you use it.

Makes 100ml

2 largish, mild, fresh red chillies, deseeded
1 tsp cumin seeds
1½ tsp coriander seeds
3 cloves
6 black peppercorns
¾ tsp turmeric
9 large cloves of garlic, peeled
1cm piece of fresh ginger, peeled
good-sized piece of cinnamon
1 tsp tamarind paste
¾ tsp sugar
¾ tsp salt
5 tbsp white wine vinegar

Blend all the ingredients together to make a fine paste. Store in a sterilized jar in the fridge for 1 week.

Making Yoghurt

Making yoghurt is the easiest thing in the world: no need for special equipment or ingredients. All you need is milk, yoghurt and a little patience. Indians from the North have always set their own yoghurt as it is used daily for raitas, making paneer or just in cooking. I do regularly make yoghurt at home, not because I want to save money, but because it has always been the way in my home and it is one of the most useful weekly recipes to do. The resulting yoghurt is fresh and sweet and sours slowly as the days pass, making a wonderful yoghurt curry at the end of its shelf life and the last dregs are used to set the next batch.

Makes 1 litre

1.2 litres milk
85ml live yoghurt

Bring the milk to the boil in a large, heavy-based pan set over a low heat, stirring and scraping the bottom frequently to prevent the milk burning and catching. Once the milk starts to bubble, cook for 8 minutes over a gentle heat. Take off the heat and leave to cool to blood temperature.

Preheat the oven to 160°C/310°F/ gas mark 2½, then turn it off.

Whisk the yoghurt so that it is lump free, and then whisk into the cooled milk so that it is completely incorporated.

Pour into a glass or ceramic container, cover and place in the oven for 8 hours. If it has not set after that time, reheat the oven for 4 minutes and turn off again. Leave until set. Store, covered, in the fridge. It should last for 5–6 days.

Paneer

Paneer is home-made, unsalted white cheese. It taste like a fresh farmer's cheese and has a dense, crumbly texture that works well either combined with spices or served simply with sea salt, freshly ground black pepper and a drizzle of good-quality olive oil. Paneer is a useful source of protein and is full of vitamins and minerals. You can buy it ready-made from the supermarket, but it is really easy to make your own.

Makes 250g

2 litres full-fat milk
200–250ml fresh yoghurt or 2 tbsp lemon juice

Bring the milk to the boil in a large heavy-based saucepan. Once the milk starts to boil and rise up, stir in 200ml of the yoghurt or all the lemon juice. Keeping the milk on the heat, stir gently to help the milk curdle – it should only take a minute or so. If it does not separate, add the rest of the yoghurt and continue stirring. The curds will coagulate and separate from the watery whey. Remove the pan from the heat.

Line a large sieve with muslin or cheesecloth and place over a large bowl or saucepan. Pour the cheese into the lined sieve and run cold water through it. Wrap the cheese in the cloth and hang it from the tap over the sink for 10 minutes to allow excess water to drain. Then, keeping it fairly tightly wrapped, place on a work surface with a heavy weight on top (I refill the same saucepan with the whey or water and place it on top) for 30–40 minutes or until it is flattened into a firm block. Then cut into cubes or crumble, depending how you want to use it.

Store unused paneer in water in a covered container in the fridge or freeze it in an airtight container (defrost thoroughly before use).

Light Meals and Snacks

Serves 3–6, depending on appetite

3 tbsp vegetable oil
1 medium onion, peeled and finely
    chopped
½ green pepper, cored and sliced
2 large cloves of garlic, peeled and
    pounded into a paste or chopped
1 tsp chopped fresh ginger
¾ tsp ground cumin
1 heaped tsp ground coriander
½–¾ tsp red chilli powder
½ tsp turmeric
salt, to taste
8 good-sized plum tomatoes, skinned (and
    seeded if you have time), chopped
2 tsp white wine vinegar
6 large eggs

Tomato-poached Eggs

These eggs are inspired by the cooking of the Parsis, who migrated to India many centuries ago from the Persia; many of them then settled in Mumbai. Amongst other things, they are known for their love of eggs and their sweet–savoury combinations. The sweetness in this dish comes from the golden onion and sweet plum tomatoes. I eat this dish for brunch or lunch and serve it with grilled rather than toasted bread, sliced from a fresh rustic loaf.

Heat the oil in a medium non-stick saucepan and fry the onion until golden. Add the green pepper and cook for 3 minutes. Add the garlic and ginger and cook, stirring, until the garlic is soft, around 1 minute. Stir in the ground spices and salt and cook for 30 seconds over a low heat.

Add the tomatoes and stir well to mix. Bring the pan to a simmer and cook, covered, for around 15–20 minutes. Taste – there should be no harsh elements. Add a splash of water from a recently boiled kettle to loosen the gravy a little, though it should still be creamy and thick. Add the vinegar and adjust the seasoning.

Smooth the surface of the mixture and make 6 hollows with the back of a spoon. Crack an egg into each hollow. Sprinkle a pinch of salt over the eggs. Cover and cook until the eggs are done to your liking, around 2–4 minutes.

2 tbsp vegetable oil
½ tsp mustard seeds
½ tsp cumin seeds
½ medium onion, peeled and chopped
1–2 green chillies, whole but pricked with
    the tip of a knife
3 large cloves of garlic, peeled and chopped
12 curry leaves
salt, to taste
½ tsp turmeric
2 tsp black masala powder (see page 12)
    or 1 tsp garam masala
250g mixed sprouted beans and lentils
1 medium tomato, chopped
1–2 tsp jaggery or brown sugar
4 tbsp desiccated coconut
1 rounded tbsp roasted peanuts (optional)

Sprouted Bean Ussal

Sprouted foods are considered extremely nutritious as they are live food. And like any other food that is growing almost up to the moment it is eaten, its nutrients have little time to deteriorate. This dish hails from Maharashtra, where they use their own version of garam masala which is a blend of roasted and powdered spices. If you do not have this spice, you can still make this dish with a standard garam masala instead, although the blends have very different characters. We used to eat this as a healthy snack between meals, as it takes little time to make. I know mothers who make this for breakfast for their children, eaten with toast. It is also served as healthy street-food on a bun, with finely chopped red onions and little crispy vermicelli-like bites called *sev*. It is a delicious dish served at any time of the day.

Heat the oil in a medium non-stick saucepan. Add the mustard and cumin seeds and, once they start popping, add the onion and green chillies and cook until the onion starts to colour, around 5 minutes. Add the garlic and curry leaves and sauté until the garlic is cooked, around 40 seconds. Stir in the salt, turmeric and black masala and cook for 1 minute over a low heat.

Add the sprouts, tomato and 200ml water. Bring to the boil, then simmer over a moderate heat for 4–6 minutes or until they are soft. Uncover and boil off most of the excess water over a high heat. Add the sugar, coconut and peanuts, if using; stir for 1 minute and serve.

Serves 2

2 boneless chicken breasts, skinned,
    pricked with a fork and slashed across
    the thicker part on the top surface
1 tbsp melted butter or vegetable oil
200g mixed salad leaves
small handful of fresh mint leaves
about 20 pistachios, skinned if possible
8–10 baby tomatoes, halved or quartered
small handful of fine green beans,
    blanched for 2 minutes

Marinade

75ml Greek yoghurt
salt, to taste
½–1 tsp red chilli powder and paprika,
    for colour
1 tsp ground cumin
6g fresh ginger, peeled and pounded into
    a paste
2 cloves of garlic, peeled and pounded
    into a paste
1 tbsp vegetable oil
¾ tsp chaat masala
1½ tsp lemon juice, or to taste
2 good pinches of dry fenugreek leaves,
    crushed in your hand
¾ tsp garam masala
½ tsp white wine vinegar

Lemon and pistachio dressing

1–1½ tbsp lemon juice
1 very small clove of garlic, peeled
15g pistachios, skinned if possible
2½ tbsp vegetable oil
salt, to taste
½ tsp freshly ground black pepper
small pinch of sugar

Chicken Tikka Salad

I love salads and it makes me sad that such a fantastic cuisine does not have more varieties of salads. Our salads are normally served alongside the other main course dishes, to provide crunch and freshness to the meal. I crave salads that are main courses in their own right, have all the textures of a meal but on one plate, and are so much lighter than a full meal. This is one of those dishes – it is a salad I have built around chicken tikka, is easy to make and you can add or take away any salad vegetables you like. The dressing is delicious and creamy, reminiscent of Caesar salad dressing in consistency but lighter and fresher. If you make the dressing in advance, it will thicken as it sits so loosen with a little water or oil and re-season to taste. The end result is delicious and satisfying without being complicated.

Whiz together the ingredients for the marinade. Tip into a non-metallic dish, add the chicken, cover with clingfilm and leave to marinate in the fridge for as long as possible – this is your chance to get the flavours into the chicken. Bring back to room temperature before continuing.

Preheat the grill. Place a baking tray on the highest shelf, as close to the grill as possible. Once hot, place the chicken on it and grill for 12 minutes, turning half-way through the cooking time. Baste with butter 2 minutes before the cooking time is up.

Meanwhile, prepare the dressing. Using a blender, make a paste of all the ingredients with 2 tablespoons of water. Taste and adjust the seasoning.

To serve, toss the salad ingredients in the dressing, pile on a plate, slice the chicken at an angle and place on top.

Serves 4 as a light meal

375g baby spinach, finely chopped
300g cooked basmati rice (cooked weight)
130g gram flour
3 tsp cumin seeds
pinch of asafoetida (optional)
¾ tsp *khar* (optional)
½ tsp red chilli powder
1–1½ tsp salt or to taste
2 tbsp vegetable oil, plus extra for greasing
¾ tsp ginger paste
¾ tsp garlic paste

Steamed Spinach and Rice Dumplings

These light, vibrant dumplings are a delicious way to eat your spinach. In India, these are called *vada* and are made into doughnut shapes with a hole in the middle, deep-fried and eaten with chutney as an afternoon snack. My mother-in-law introduced me to her way of steaming them, and, in typical Indian manner, makes them using leftover ingredients. The original version is flavoured with *khar* – this is the distinctive but indescribable flavour found in poppadoms. It is sold as a powder in Indian shops, but do not buy it just for this recipe. If you have some already, this is the dish to use it in; if you do not have any, make it without – the dumplings are still delicious and are a meal in themselves with rice, greens and protein from the gram flour. We eat them with plain, seasoned yoghurt on the side. You will need a steamer of sorts, either bamboo steamers stacked on top of each other or a fan steamer.

Fill a large saucepan with water to a depth of 4cm and bring to the boil. Place a steamer basket on top, preferably one that stacks so you can steam all the dumplings at the same time. Oil a plate that will fit inside the steamer.

Place all the ingredients into a deep bowl and mix together well with your hands. You will need to squeeze the mixture well to help the spinach release its water which will bind the whole thing together. This takes about 5–6 minutes. Taste and adjust the seasoning.

Divide the mixture into 12 portions. Form these into balls, flatten slightly and place on the steamer plate. Place the plate in the steamer basket, cover tightly with a lid and steam for 15 minutes or until a toothpick inserted into the centre of one comes out clean.

Serve hot with seasoned thick-set yoghurt.

Tiffin

An army cannot march on an empty stomach and the same can be said for us ordinary folk. For generations, Indian wives have cooked meals for their husbands and sent it to them for lunch. The word 'tiffin' is a British word for a light lunch and came with the Raj to India. The terminology was adopted by Indians and soon came to mean any type of packed lunch. Depending on the region, this could consist of a cooked vegetable dish, a curry, rice or bread, and a sweet or savoury snack. These are all placed in separate containers or compartments, then stacked on top of each other and lowered into an insulated container.

The tiffin still survives in India today, most famously in Mumbai, where hundreds of thousands of meals are made at home and handed over to dabbawallas, 'men who handle boxes'. The container is colour coded and transported with other tiffins on wooden carts from a local collection point to the railway station. From here it is passed, relay-style, to the next set of dabbawallas who will take them to the city and the last leg of the journey sees them delivered to the correct office on the correct floor of the correct building with unbelievable accuracy. They arrive hot, just in time for lunch.

My mother always sent a tiffin with my father for lunch – take-aways or restaurant food did not appeal to men of his generation. More recently, a friend of mine started to send a tiffin with her banker husband in Manhattan. Within a month she was making twenty tiffins a day for his colleagues.

We do have a tradition of tiffin in the UK, only it is for our children in the form of school lunch boxes and unfortunately, as we all know, this is a dying trend. Personally, I love the idea of tiffin: fresh, healthy food ready to hand whenever and wherever hunger strikes. I know it isn't easy to find time to prepare food ahead, but food for your tiffin could be cooked at night as you make dinner (hopefully you are cooking at some point!) and reheated the following day. I know it is easier said than done, but no pain, no gain!

The best way of getting started is to dive right in. Start off with a few simple recipes from the first chapter, such as the Sprouted Bean Ussal (see page 18), Chicken Tikka Salad (see page 21), Mini Corn Cakes (see page 28) and Anglo-Indian Tomato Soup (see page 41), or a lentil dish (see pages 170–189), which you can eat with some fresh bread. Enjoy!

Serves 8

300g paneer (made from 1.75 litres milk,
    see page 13), diced into 3cm cubes
    or larger rectangles
oil, for greasing
2 tbsp melted butter, for basting

Marinade

120ml double cream
100ml Greek yoghurt
35g fresh mint leaves
1–3 green chillies, deseeded
1 tsp garam masala
1$\frac{1}{2}$ tsp fennel seeds, ground to a powder
$\frac{1}{2}$ tsp green cardamom powder
$\frac{1}{2}$ tsp carom seeds
$\frac{1}{2}$ tsp ground cumin
1 tbsp gram flour
4 tsp lemon juice, or to taste
salt, to taste

Delicate Mint Paneer Tikka

Paneer tikkas are a great pre-dinner appetizer to make for a group of friends who are waiting for dinner. A vegetarian starter that is neither too heavy nor too potent a flavour and caters for both vegetarians and non-vegetarians is a great choice. This recipe is so easy, even if you make your own paneer. It only requires whizzing the marinade ingredients together and then placing the dish in the oven once your guests arrive. Mint is the dominant flavour but is not overpowering. I have left out the garlic and ginger pastes that would usually be added to a tandoori dish because I wanted the flavours to remain delicate and light. If you wish, skewer cubes of red onion and pepper (blanch well first) between the paneer and serve with a side salad or some coriander and mint chutney (see page 218).

Blend together all the marinade ingredients with 3–4 tablespoons of water. Taste and adjust the seasoning, chillies and lemon juice to taste.

Tip the marinade into a non-metallic bowl and add the paneer. Cover with clingfilm and leave in the fridge to marinate for a few hours.

Preheat the oven to 190°C/375°F/gas mark 5 and oil a baking tray. Bring the paneer back to room temperature. Arrange the paneer cubes on the tray – the marinade is quite thick so it will cling to the paneer. Place on the upper shelf in the oven and bake for 8 minutes, turning halfway through the cooking time. Baste with butter and bake for another minute. The paneer cubes should be slightly browning at the edges. Serve hot.

Makes 8

4 tbsp vegetable oil
1 small onion, peeled and chopped
1 fat clove of garlic, peeled and grated
    or crushed
190g potato, boiled, peeled and mashed
1 green chilli, deseeded and finely chopped
2 tbsp finely chopped red pepper
1 tsp ground cumin
¾ tsp caraway seeds
30g Cheddar cheese, grated
salt, to taste
200g canned sweetcorn, drained and rinsed
3 rounded tbsp gram flour
coriander and mint chutney, to serve
    (see page 218)

Red chilli crème fraîche (optional)

2 mild red chillies, deseeded
salt, to taste
½–¾ tsp lemon juice, or to taste
4 tbsp low-fat crème fraîche
¼ tsp garlic paste

Mini Corn Cakes

Mild, slightly sweet, slightly savoury and with a little punch from the chillies, these corn cakes are delicious little bites to kickstart your evening. They are so easy to make and take just minutes to cook. Serve with coriander and mint chutney, topped with a little red chilli crème fraîche if you wish, or just a small dollop of sour cream and a sprinkling of chopped tomatoes and mild red chillies.

Heat 2 teaspoons of the oil in a frying pan and fry the onion until soft and golden. Add the garlic and cook for 30 seconds. Take off the heat and place in a bowl. Add the potato, chilli, red pepper, spices, cheese and salt.

Squeeze out as much liquid from the corn as possible. Purée three-quarters of the corn in a blender and add both this and the whole kernels to the onion mixture.

Place the gram flour in a dry pan and stir-fry until the flour turns a shade darker and emits its distinctive smell, around 2–3 minutes. Mix into the corn. Using clean hands, make 8 cakes with the mixture.

Next, make the red chilli crème fraîche, if using. Using a pestle and mortar, make a fine paste of the red chillies with a little of the salt and some lemon juice. Stir into the crème fraîche with the garlic paste. Taste and adjust the amounts of salt and lemon juice.

Heat the remaining oil in a large non-stick frying pan. Add the corn cakes to the pan and cook over a low heat until the bottoms have turned golden. Turn over and brown the other side. Place on a plate lined with kitchen paper.

Serve hot with a generous dollop of the coriander and mint chutney on top, and finish with a spoonful of the red chilli crème fraîche, if using.

Makes 20

4 black cardamom pods and 16 green
    cardamom pods, bashed using a
    pestle and mortar, seeds kept and
    husks discarded
8 cloves
1cm piece of cinnamon stick
500g lamb mince, extra finely minced
    (ask your butcher to mince it three times)
1 medium egg
½ tsp turmeric
½–1 tsp red chilli powder
½ tsp ground cumin
1 large slice of white bread, crusts
    removed and crumbed
2 tbsp Greek yoghurt
1 rounded tsp ginger paste
salt, to taste (I add 1¾ tsp)
3 tbsp vegetable oil
coriander and mint chutney or radish
    and yoghurt chutney (see page 218),
    to serve

Kashmiri Lamb Kebabs

As well as avoiding meat, strict vegetarians in old India would often shun onion and garlic too, as these were all thought to imbue the person eating them with a character probably best described as 'animalistic', something the spiritually-inclined Hindus wanted to avoid. Most Hindus continue to be vegetarian and many still avoid garlic and onions. The Hindus of Kashmir are unusual in that their cuisine has evolved over the centuries to incorporate many types of meat, but the dishes are still cooked without onions and garlic. This is one of those dishes and, in the absence of stronger flavours, the spices are able to shine and give these delicious kebabs all they need in terms of flavouring. Here I have used a non-stick pan to cook the small patties, but in the summer you could make long kebabs on skewers and grill them on the barbecue for an extra charcoal flavour. Serve them as an appetizer with drinks with radish and yoghurt chutney or coriander and mint chutney.

Grind the whole spices to a fine powder and tip into a large bowl with the mince, egg, powdered spices, breadcrumbs, yoghurt, ginger paste and salt. Mix well with your hands

Divide into 20 portions and make into small, disc-like kebabs or patties.

Heat 1½ tablespoons of the oil in a large non-stick frying pan and fry half the kebabs on a low heat until browned on both sides and cooked through the middle, around 3 minutes on each side. Repeat with the second batch. Serve hot with the chutney.

Makes about 16 small pieces

4 slices of white bread (medium cut is best), crusts removed, or 16 slices cut from a small, thin baguette
5 tbsp vegetable oil
1 small onion, peeled and finely chopped
2 tsp chopped fresh ginger
3 large cloves of garlic, peeled and finely chopped

1–3 thin green chillies, chopped
salt, to taste
¾ tsp ground cumin
¾ tsp ground coriander
1 large tomato, chopped
300g small raw prawns, peeled and cleaned
2 tbsp chopped fresh coriander
4 tbsp fresh breadcrumbs
2 large eggs, whisked with 2 tbsp milk and a pinch of salt

Prawn Toasts

These familiar-sounding snacks are indeed similar to Chinese fried prawn toasts. This particular recipe hails from Goa, a region strongly influenced by the Portuguese, who were the first settlers on the island of Macau and stayed there for centuries before handing the island to the Chinese on the eve of this millennium. I am sure these prawn toasts were brought by the Portuguese first to China and then on to India, adopting the flavours of each region as, at the time, bread was alien to both cultures. These toasts are absolutely delicious and taste of India rather than any other country. I like to serve bite-sized portions as a pre-dinner snack with drinks, but they also work well equally as a starter with a salad or as a light meal.

Toast the slices of bread in a toaster until crisp. Cut diagonally into quarters.

Heat 2 tablespoons of the oil in a small non-stick saucepan and fry the onion until pale golden. Add the ginger, garlic, chillies and salt and stir-fry for 30 seconds. Add a splash of water and cook until dry. Add the spices and tomato and cook for 4 minutes. Add the prawns and stir-fry until just cooked, about 2–3 minutes. There should be no extra water in the pan; if there is, dry off over a high heat. Taste and adjust the seasoning, if necessary. Stir in the chopped coriander and breadcrumbs.

Take heaped teaspoons of the filling and press firmly onto the pieces of toast.

Heat about 1½ tablespoons of the oil in a large non-stick frying pan to a moderate heat. Dip half the toasts, topping side down, in the egg so that it coats only the topping and not the whole toast. Place the toasts, egg-side down, in the oil. Fry for 2–3 minutes or until the egg has set. At this stage you can remove the toasts and serve or turn them over and fry the undersides too. This does enhance the taste, but the toasts will be that bit heavier (you will also need more oil). Repeat with the remaining oil and toasts. Serve on their own or with some red chilli and coconut chutney (see page 222).

Makes around 18 cocktail cakes

5 cloves
2cm piece of cinnamon
1½ tsp cumin seeds
5 tbsp vegetable oil
1 small–medium onion, peeled and chopped
5 large cloves of garlic, peeled and chopped
1 tbsp chopped ginger

salt, to taste
½–¾ tsp red chilli powder
1 tsp garam masala
1½–2 tsp dried mango powder
450g fish fillets, such as salmon, trout, cod or haddock
15g fresh coriander leaves and stalks, chopped
1 large egg, beaten
60–70g fresh breadcrumbs (about 2 large slices), to bind

Spiced Fish Cakes

Indians often eat fish cakes in the form of bite-sized morsels before dinner – just enough to whet their appetite for the main meal but not so filling as to compromise the main course. These bites are flavourful, light and not too spicy. Many regions have their own version, but I think a good way of changing the flavours would be to serve them with different, tangy chutneys. You can also add to their texture by dipping them in flour and egg and crumbing them before frying, for a crisper finish. These cakes work really well with many types of fish – I love them made with salmon or trout, but any white fish fillets can be used. Serve with the coriander and mint chutney or quick red chilli and coconut chutney for a change (see pages 218 and 222).

Grind together the cloves, cinnamon and cumin seeds to a fine powder.

Heat 2 tablespoons of the oil in a small non-stick frying pan and fry the onion until golden. Add the garlic and ginger and cook, stirring, over a low heat, for 50–60 seconds. Add the salt and all the spices; cook for another 20 seconds.

Meanwhile, cook the fish in a pan in just enough water to cover until just opaque – this takes just 2–4 minutes depending on the thickness of the fillets. Drain on kitchen paper and flake into pieces.

Mix together the spiced onion mixture, fish and coriander. Taste and adjust the chilli, salt and dried mango powder (for tartness). Stir in the egg and then the breadcrumbs to bind. Use as much as you need for soft cakes that will hold their shape. Form into small, flat cakes.

Heat half the remaining oil in a large non-stick pan. Add half the cakes and fry over a lowish heat until both sides have browned, around 2 minutes per side. Repeat with the remaining oil and cakes. Serve hot with chutney.

Serves 2

3 slices of bread, lightly toasted until hard
    but not coloured, crusts removed
1 tbsp natural yoghurt (slightly sour if
    possible)
2 tbsp vegetable oil
¼ tsp brown mustard seeds
1 small–medium onion, peeled and finely
    sliced
1 small potato, peeled and chopped into
    1cm cubes
1 green chilli, deseeded and chopped
    or slit
1 large carrot, peeled and grated into long
    shreds
¼ small red or white cabbage, cored and
    finely shredded
1 rounded tsp ginger paste
salt, to taste
1½–2 tsp lemon juice, or to taste
2 tbsp chopped fresh coriander leaves
    and stalks

Quick Bread and Vegetable Stir-fry

This simple dish makes a wonderfully healthy quick snack or light meal. There are no spices in this dish, just a delicious combination of sweet vegetables with a bite and the soft, tart pieces of bread. It may not sound like much, but it just works. If the yoghurt is slightly sour with age and the bread not as fresh as it could be, so much the better. A great store-cupboard recipe, this is a typical example of how Indians took a staple ingredient from another culture and made it their own. I use wholemeal bread as this is what I have at home and it has a nutty flavour I am used to, but use whichever you have to hand.

Cut each slice of bread into 9 squares. Brush the yoghurt on both sides of the toast and leave on a plate in a single layer to dry off a little.

Heat the oil in a large non-stick frying pan and fry the mustard seeds until they start to pop. Add the onion and fry until golden, around 6 minutes. Stir in the potato and continue frying over a moderate heat until nearly cooked, around 5–6 minutes. Add the green chilli, followed by the carrot, cabbage, ginger paste and salt, then stir-fry for 5–6 minutes or until they have wilted.

Stir in the lemon juice and bread and cook for another 2 minutes. Taste and adjust the seasoning, sprinkle over the coriander and serve.

Serves 4

1 tbsp butter
1 tsp vegetable oil
1 large bay leaf
1 medium onion, peeled and chopped
1 large carrot, peeled and sliced
1 celery stalk, sliced
2 cloves of garlic, peeled and sliced
8g fresh ginger, peeled and roughly
    chopped
1 tbsp cornflour
650g ripe tomatoes, chopped
$^3/_4$–1 tsp sugar (depending on tomatoes)
salt, to taste
$^3/_4$–1 tsp freshly ground black pepper
100ml milk

Coriander and garlic bread

30g fresh coriander, leaves and stalks
3 tbsp vegetable oil
1 small clove of garlic, peeled
salt, to taste
4 slices of bread – I use a rustic loaf or
    baguette, sliced on the diagonal

Anglo-Indian Tomato Soup

I love the idea of the natural evolution of food as much as I love learning about the provenance and history of original dishes. This dish was introduced into India by the British at the time of the Raj and is reminiscent of cream of tomato soup but with more flavour. Soup is rarely seen in India, although it sometimes appears in the south as a watery, peppery concoction, sometimes in restaurants as *shorbas* and on cold days in the north as a small mug of soup to sip mid-evening to ward off the cold. I love this soup either with a hunk of fresh wholegrain bread or one of my favourite accompaniments, a thick slice of coriander and garlic bread. When making the bread, the oil will discolour if left too long, so make when you are going to use it.

Heat the butter and oil in a large non-stick saucepan, add the bay leaf and cook for 20 seconds. Add the onion, carrot, celery, garlic and ginger. Cover and cook gently for around 10–12 minutes until the vegetables have softened and the onions are colouring.

Add the cornflour and stir for 1–2 minutes; it shouldn't colour. Add the tomatoes, sugar, salt and black pepper and cook for 20–30 minutes or until the tomatoes have completely reduced to a thick mass. Then spend 5–6 minutes 'browning' the reduced tomatoes – this will add depth to the curry.

Meanwhile, to make the coriander and garlic bread, put the coriander, oil, garlic and salt in a blender and whiz to a sloppy paste with small bits of coriander still whole. Heat a ridged griddle pan. Grill the bread, not moving it once you have placed the slices on the pan so they have charred lines running across them. Turn and repeat on the other side. (You can also do this is in the oven.) Remove and brush over a generous amount of the coriander and garlic oil.

Take out the bay leaf and purée the soup with a little water until smooth. Add the milk and enough water to get that luscious cream-of-tomato consistency. Bring to the boil and serve with the coriander and garlic bread.

Serves 6

180ml natural yoghurt
150g gram flour
1–2 thin green chillies, deseeded
8g fresh ginger, peeled
1 tbsp vegetable oil
2½–3 tbsp lemon juice (if your yoghurt is
    quite fresh, add the extra)
½ tsp turmeric
salt, to taste
1 tsp sugar, or to taste
¾ tsp fruit salts (see page 250)
quick tamarind chutney (see page 222),
    to serve

Topping

1½ tbsp vegetable oil
1 tsp mustard seeds
1½ tsp sesame seeds
12 curry leaves
1 tsp sugar
handful of fresh grated coconut and
    chopped coriander, to garnish

Spongy Lentil Cake

This light, spongy snack, hailing from Gujarat, is definitely a national institution. In India it is as popular as the samosa, pakora or bhaji and makes a perfect afternoon snack. However, it is easier to make, gratifyingly moreish and full of clean flavours, yet it is as light as a feather; you can eat a plate-full and still go out for a meal. I don't know anyone who doesn't like this cake. This recipe is a quick and easy version as the traditional one would be made with lentils soaked overnight and ground to a paste. You do need to have something suitable to steam the cake in – typically a steel plate with high sides is used, but a sandwich tin will also do the trick. The cake is also great served with quick tamarind chutney (see page 222).

Whisk the yoghurt into the flour in a generous bowl to get a smooth, lump-free batter.

Oil a 15–18cm sandwich tin. Fill the saucepan of a double boiler with water and bring to the boil. Alternatively, place a trivet or a small heatproof bowl (I use a large biscuit cutter or steel pudding bowl) in a large, deep saucepan and fill with enough water to come half way up the trivet. This is to keep the plate above the water, allowing the cake to steam without direct contact with the hot water. Bring to the boil.

Using a blender, make a paste with the chillies, ginger, oil, lemon juice and 30ml water. Stir into the batter along with the turmeric, salt and sugar – it should be slightly sweet, salty and tart. Adjust if necessary. Stir in the fruit salts and leave for 5 minutes. Pour into the tin – the batter should come about three-quarters of the way up the side. Place the tin in the pan, cover with a lid and steam over a moderate heat for 18–20 minutes or until a toothpick inserted into the cake comes out clean.

To make the topping, heat the oil in a small pan. Add the mustard seeds and when they start to pop, add the sesame seeds and curry leaves. Once the sesame seeds colour, add 4 tablespoons of water and the sugar. Boil for 2 minutes, then pour evenly over the cake. Cut into wedges or 5cm squares or diamond shapes and garnish with the fresh coriander and coconut.

Goan Chorizo Sandwich

Serves 2

1 tbsp vegetable oil
1 medium–large onion, peeled, halved and sliced
salt
1 Goan chorizo, sliced into 2cm pieces
large handful of rocket
4 thick slices from a large loaf of bread

Goan chorizo is a wonderful smoky, spicy sausage of a medium–hard consistency. It is often added to Goan rice dishes, as well as to their stews and casseroles. I think it is great in these delicious, warm sandwiches, with the onions adding a caramelized sweetness and the rocket a fresh, peppery counterpoint. It isn't so easy to find these sausages, but try looking in specialist delis and food shops.

Heat the oil in a small non-stick pan. Add the onion and a little salt (not too much, as there is some in the sausage) and cook until golden brown. Add the sliced chorizo and stir-fry for 4 minutes over a moderate–high heat, adding a splash of water halfway. The chorizo slices should release their oil into the onions and cook through.

Place the rocket on two slices of bread, top with the cooked onions and chorizo, then with the remaining slices of bread, and get stuck in!

Opposite: Goan Chorizo Sandwich

Raw Banana Chips

Makes enough for 4 to munch on

2 raw, green bananas, peeled and
    thinly sliced
vegetable oil, for frying
salt, to taste
$\frac{1}{8}$–$\frac{1}{4}$ tsp red chilli powder
$\frac{1}{4}$ tsp turmeric

Raw bananas are green in colour and the starch has not yet turned to sugar, so the fruit is treated like a starchy vegetable. In this state, the banana is considered very healthy and contains lots of calcium. Here it is sliced very thinly and fried (as you would with crisps), then seasoned and dusted with red chilli powder. The chips are very moreish and have more texture than potato chips, with the chilli adding a warming kick. You will find green bananas in Asian markets and you do have to use them before they ripen. The skin will not peel off as it would with a yellow banana, so use a knife to remove it, keeping the banana as round as possible.

Peel the bananas using a knife. Slice thinly, as you would for potato crisps.

Heat the oil in a large deep frying pan. Add half the banana chips or as many as will sit in one layer. Fry over a low heat until the edges are golden and crisp, around 5 minutes, turning often. Mix $\frac{1}{2}$ teaspoon of salt with $\frac{1}{2}$ teaspoon of water and the turmeric and carefully pour it into the hot oil; stir well. Continue frying for another minute or so.

Spoon out the chips, draining as much oil as possible, and place on kitchen paper. Sprinkle over the chilli powder and toss to mix. Repeat until you have used up all the bananas. Eat hot or cold.

Fish and Seafood

20g fresh ginger, peeled
6 large cloves of garlic, peeled
1½ tsp fennel seeds
4 tbsp coconut or vegetable oil
¾ tsp cumin seeds
¾ tsp mustard seeds
¼ tsp fenugreek seeds
100g shallots or onion, peeled and finely
    chopped
salt, to taste
12 large curry leaves
¼–½ tsp red chilli powder, or to taste
1 tsp ground coriander
1 tsp garam masala
2 thin green chillies (optional)
½–¾ tsp tamarind paste, or to taste
450g fish, either steaks or fillets (salt the
    fillets earlier to make them firmer)

Kerala's Red Fish Curry

Fish and spices are synonymous with the southern region of Kerala. The resulting seafood dishes are wonderfully fresh, spicy and often fiery. This is one of those dishes, one the fishermen would make themselves. The red comes from the red chilli, which you can add to taste. The flavours themselves are wonderful and, if you wish, you can add a spoon of coconut cream to temper the spices. When I hear people's concerns of pairing fish with spices, I sometimes wonder how the Indian fishermen would react if they heard it. That something so natural is questioned would be hard for them to believe. I'm sure they would shrug it off, laugh and tuck into the freshest and tastiest fish curry. This recipe works well with any flavourful, firm fish, such as red mullet, mackerel or sardines.

Using a blender, make a fine paste of the ginger, garlic and fennel seeds with 100ml water.

Heat the oil in large non-stick saucepan, then add the cumin seeds and mustard seeds. Once they start to pop, add the fenugreek seeds and cook for 20 seconds. Add the chopped shallots and cook until golden. Add the ginger paste, salt, the remaining spices and the green chillies, if using. Bring to a boil, then simmer for 20 minutes. You may need to add a little more water if the pan becomes dry.

When dry again, add 200ml water and the tamarind, bring to the boil and stir well to mix. Add the fish, bring back to the boil and cook gently for another 4–6 minutes, then serve.

Serves 8–10 with a side salad

Filling
3 tbsp vegetable oil
2 onions, peeled and sliced
3 large cloves of garlic, peeled
6g fresh ginger, peeled
6–8 mild dried red chillies
1 piece of cinnamon stick

5 black peppercorns
4 cloves
¾ tsp cumin seeds
salt, to taste
2 medium tomatoes, chopped
2½ tsp sugar, or to taste
2 tbsp white wine vinegar, or to taste
300g raw prawns, peeled and
    deveined

Batter
100g sugar
120g butter, at room temperature
3 large eggs and 1 extra yolk
¾ tsp salt
240g plain flour
1 tsp baking powder
175ml milk
100g desiccated coconut
80g semolina, soaked in 125ml water
    for 15 minutes

Goan Prawn Cake

This is an old Goan dish that many have already forgotten about and locals are worried it might soon become obsolete as newer, faster recipes encroach on the New India. When I heard about this dish, I was intrigued and read up on it some more. It is a really unusual taste combination – a sweet yet savoury filling of prawns is baked inside a sweet coconut cake. It is reminiscent of Chinese dim sum pork buns, where the filling is both sweet and savoury and the bun is a sweet, yeast bread. I am sure both were the influence of the Portuguese as bread was neither Chinese nor Indian, but much loved by the Portuguese. Indians made it theirs with the local prawns and spices. I'm not sure if this dish will appeal to the masses, but I think it is delicious and relevant to the history of Goa and, as such, I'm sad to see it disappearing from use. The prawn filling can be made the day before and brought back to room temperature before baking.

Heat the oil in a medium sized non-stick saucepan. Add the onions and fry until golden. Meanwhile, using a blender, make a fine paste of the garlic and ginger with a little water. Grind the chillies and spices to a fine powder. Add the spices and salt to the pan and stir over a low heat for 20 seconds. Add the paste and cook for 2–3 minutes or until the raw smell of garlic has disappeared. Add the tomatoes and a splash of water and cook, covered, for 15 minutes, or until they have completely broken down. Give the pot an occasional stir and mash the tomato pieces down a little.

Stir in the sugar and vinegar and cook for 2–3 minutes; the masala should be quite thick. Add the prawns and cook until they have just turned and start to curl up, around 3–4 minutes. Remove from the heat and cool.

Grease a round, deep 20–23cm cake tin and preheat the oven to 200°C/400°F/gas mark 6.

To make the batter, beat together the sugar and butter until soft and creamy. Beat in the eggs one at a time, making sure each is fully incorporated before adding the next. Add the remaining ingredients and mix well. The batter should have a thick, dropping consistency.

Spoon half the batter into the cake tin. Spread the filling over it, distributing the prawns evenly. Pour the remaining batter over the top and bake in the middle of the oven for 55–60 minutes or until a toothpick inserted into the centre comes out clean and dry. Serve in wedges with a lightly dressed salad.

Serves 4–6

2 tbsp vegetable oil
1 medium onion, peeled and chopped
14 large curry leaves
2–4 green chillies, left whole but pricked
    with the point of a knife
salt, to taste
400ml coconut milk
1 small green mango, cut in half (the stone
    is still soft), stone removed, flesh
    peeled and chopped into small pieces
600g white fish fillets, cut into large chunks
$\frac{1}{2}$ tsp garam masala

Spice paste

5 large cloves of garlic, peeled
12g fresh ginger, peeled and halved
$1\frac{1}{2}$ tsp cumin seeds
1 tbsp coriander seeds or ground coriander
$\frac{1}{4}$ tsp turmeric

Fish and Green Mango Curry

This is a fabulous creamy curry from Kerala. Although fish is obviously the main ingredient, for me the star is the mango. As spring approaches, the arrival of the king of Indian fruits is anticipated by all. But before the mango grows into the sweet, luscious orange fruit we know and love, it is small, green, hard and sour. Yet even in this state the mangoes are sought after for their tartness and health-giving properties. This is one of those dishes that showcases the mango's versatility. If the season is yet to come or there are no green mangoes in your vicinity, local Keralans simply add tamarind or cocum (another sour fruit) instead to provide the same function.

Place all the ingredients for the spice paste into a blender, add about 50ml water and blend to a fine paste.

Heat the oil in a large non-stick saucepan. Add the onion and fry until browned. Stir in the curry leaves and green chillies and cook for 10 seconds. Add the paste and salt and cook over a moderate heat, stirring occasionally, until completely reduced. Then fry the paste gently, stirring, for a further 2–3 minutes.

Add the coconut milk, 300ml water and the green mango pieces. Bring to the boil, cover and simmer over a moderate heat for 20 minutes or until the mango pieces have broken down. Taste and adjust the seasoning.

Add the fish and garam masala and cook for 3–4 minutes or until the fish is just cooked through. If the curry has thickened too much, add a splash of boiling water from a recently boiled kettle and shake the pan to mix. Serve with plain rice.

Serves 2 (can easily be doubled)

2 tbsp mustard oil or 1 tbsp each butter and oil
½ tsp panch phoran (see page 249)
2 small cloves of garlic, peeled and thinly sliced
1–2 green chillies, left whole but pricked with the point of a knife
salt, to taste
2 tbsp white poppy seeds, ground to a fine powder in a spice grinder
⅛ tsp red chilli powder
½ tsp garam masala
2 trout fillets
1½ tsp lemon juice or to taste
handful of fresh coriander, chopped

Trout with White Poppy Seeds

This unusual dish is something I had wanted to create for at least eight months before I actually went out and bought the trout from my local fishmonger. Bengalis use a lot of poppy seeds with their vegetables and I absolutely love their nutty flavour. I grew up eating trout cooked with butter and almonds and loved the sweet-flavoured fish with the buttery, lemony juice. I really wanted to try to make an Indian version of a nutty fish, and this is the culmination of that inspiration. Bengalis will tell you it is not traditional (I have added no sugar) but, on the whole, the flavours are wholly theirs and could easily be cooked by an adventurous local. Serve with steaming hot rice or simple mashed potatoes to soak up all the delicious juices.

Heat the oil in a wide non-stick frying pan until smoking, then allow to cool for 15 seconds. Add the panch phoran and fry for 10–15 seconds or until starting to pop. Stir in the garlic, green chillies and salt and cook until the garlic is starting to colour. Stir in the poppy seed powder, red chilli powder and garam masala. Cook for 20 seconds or until the seeds start to brown. Add 100ml water and cook, stirring occasionally, until the liquid has dried off.

Add the fish with a splash of water and shake the pan to incorporate. Cook, covered, for 3–4 minutes or until the fish is cooked through. Drizzle with the lemon juice, stir in the coriander and serve.

Love crispy skin? For a crisp skin, use only half the oil in the beginning. Then, once the sauce is ready, remove from the pan and place in a bowl. Give the pan a wipe with kitchen paper and add the remaining oil, heat until smoking, then take the pan off the heat. Dredge the trout in seasoned flour and place, skin-side down. Give the pan a shake and cook the fish undisturbed for 2 minutes, turn it over and cook for another minute. Place on your plates, return the sauce to the pan, add a small splash of water and swirl to pick up the flavours of the trout and make a light gravy. Stir in the lemon juice and coriander and spoon around the fish.

West Bengal

West Bengal is known for its intellectuals, artists, musicians and poets but not yet for its food. On my first visit to Kolkota five years ago, I was curious about this elusive cuisine, so went to a recommended restaurant, Kewpie's, where I was served a traditional meal. A plate with rice, salt, chilli and lime is placed in front of you. Then a succession of dishes arrives, each served by itself and eaten solely with rice, so the flavours of each dish are enjoyed as they were meant to be. First comes a fried vegetable and a bowl of lentils, then a vegetable dish, followed by fish. Seafood is next, then a meat or chicken dish, a sweet and sour chutney, and finally a dessert. Each course has a stronger flavour than the last. This is a sophisticated cuisine that has been well thought out.

Bengalis are, at heart, fish eaters – fried, boiled, poached, steamed, flaked, crumbed or cooked in a bubbling broth. The heads are added to vegetable dishes; the bones and tails used in stir-fries. It is relished in its entirety. Other essential Bengali ingredients are mustard oil, which they cook with,

and mustard seeds, crushed into a paste with water to make the freshest wholegrain mustard. They love these ingredients and use them in combinations that no one else would ever dare to do – proof of the independent nature of this region.

Bengal's tables were further enriched, albeit inadvertently, in the reign of the Raj. The memsahibs, unused to the strong new flavours, taught their cooks dishes from their world. The result was a natural hybrid that was neither Eastern nor Western – kedgeree, spiced croquettes of all types, pantaras (pancakes) stuffed with leftover spiced-up roast, spicy fish fingers and Armenian-style stuffed vegetables. For a taste of the new and old flavours of Bengal, try Anglo-Indian Tomato Soup (see page 41), Trout with White Poppy Seeds (see page 55), Coconut and Mustard Prawns (see page 68), Bengali Fish Stew (see page 73), Indian Shepherd's Pie (see page 115), Bengali Squash with Chickpeas (see page 151) and Spiced Poached Peaches (see page 226).

2 tbsp vegetable oil
1 tsp mustard seeds
1 small onion, peeled and chopped
2.5cm piece of cinnamon stick
10g fresh ginger, peeled
7 large cloves of garlic, peeled
1–3 mild dried red chillies
1 tsp ground cumin
2 tsp ground coriander
$\frac{1}{2}$ tsp turmeric
$\frac{1}{2}$ tsp garam masala
2 medium tomatoes, puréed
400ml coconut milk
450g firm white fish fillets, cut into
    large cubes
salt, to taste, and lots of freshly ground
    black pepper

Goan Fish Curry

There are so many types of fish curries in Goa and this is one of the most popular ones.
It delivers everything a curry should – layers of flavour, depth, tartness and a hint of
sweetness from the onion and coconut. It is delicious and beautiful and lends itself to
a variety of seafood and not just fish – try making it with prawns, mussels, clams or squid,
if you wish. I sometimes add green chillies at the end for that added pungency and also for
colour, but you can leave them out. While on the subject of chillies, most Indian stores sell
packets of dried red chillies from different regions of India, each with different heat. Ask
them for something mild – I often opt for chillies from Kashmir but can personally take even
medium heat chillies in this quantity. If you know you can't take heat, you can add some red
chilli powder to taste towards the end of cooking or a little paprika powder to mimic that
beautiful peachy-red colour.

Heat the vegetable oil in a large non-stick saucepan. Add the mustard seeds and, once they are popping, turn the
heat down and add the onion and cinnamon. Cook the onion until golden, around 8 minutes.

Meanwhile, using a blender, make a fine paste of the ginger, garlic and chillies with 50ml water. Add this to the
cooked onions along with the powdered spices. Cook until reduced, then fry over a low heat for 2 minutes or until
the oil is released. Add the tomatoes and another 100ml water; cook until completely reduced and fry the paste for
4–5 minutes or until the oil comes out on top.

Stir in the coconut milk and 150ml water, bring to a gentle simmer and allow the flavours to marry and develop for
5 minutes. Add the fish and cook until done, around 4–5 minutes. Taste and adjust the seasoning, then serve.

Makes 2 fillets (can easily be doubled)

2 sole fillets
3 tbsp vegetable oil
crusty rolls, salad leaves and lemon
    wedges, to serve

Marinade

2 tsp lemon juice
$^3/_4$ tsp ginger paste
$^1/_2$ tsp garlic paste
$^1/_4$ tsp freshly ground black pepper
$^1/_4$ tsp salt

Batter

50g gram flour
$^3/_4$ tsp ginger paste
1$^1/_2$ tsp garlic paste
1 tsp carom seeds
1–2 dried red chillies (medium heat) or
    red chilli powder, to taste
$^1/_2$ tsp baking powder
salt, to taste

Battered Amritsari Sole

A dish has to be special to be named after its provenance; this one is. It is named after the Punjabi city of Amritsar in which it gained fame. The city is known primarily for its magnificent golden temple, but it has become a destination for food lovers of many backgrounds. The people of Punjab are known to have a joie de vivre – a love of life, food, music, dance and drink. This city showcases how their love of food translates into some of the best dishes in the land. This dish is normally deep-fried and served with coriander and mint chutney with pre-dinner drinks, almost like Indian tapas. However, I like to batter up large fillets, pan-fry them and serve on a bed of salad in a crusty roll, with a generous slick of the chutney and with or without mayo, depending on mood.

Combine the ingredients for the marinade in a non-metallic bowl. Place the fish in the marinade and leave for 30 minutes, then remove and pat dry.

Meanwhile, blend together all the ingredients for the batter with 60ml cold water. It should have a thick, coating consistency. Taste for salt and chilli.

Heat the oil in a non-stick frying pan until hot. Dip the fish in the batter and place in the frying pan. Once the bottom has browned and crisped up, around 40–50 seconds, turn over and repeat with the other side. Once golden, remove from the pan and drain on kitchen paper before serving.

Serves 4–6

5 tbsp vegetable oil
4 cloves
2 black cardamom pods
5cm piece of cinnamon stick
1 small–medium onion, peeled and
    chopped
5 large cloves of garlic, peeled
10g fresh ginger, peeled
1–2 green chillies, left whole but pricked
    with the tip of a knife
½ tsp turmeric

½ tsp red chilli powder, or to taste
1 rounded tsp ground cumin
1 rounded tsp ground coriander
1½ tsp garam masala
½ tsp freshly ground black pepper
salt, to taste
4 medium tomatoes, puréed
50g cashew nuts, made into a paste with
    some water
500g fish steaks or fillets, cut into large
    chunks
handful of fresh coriander, leaves and
    stalks, chopped

Creamy North Indian Fish Curry

This is a rich northern fish curry that uses cashew nuts to thicken and enrich the gravy. It is a smooth and creamy dish that is more of a restaurant dish than home-cooked, and is great with naan and pilaffs. I know the list of ingredients looks long but, really, most of these will be added in quick and easy succession. You do need to have patience to wait for the masala to cook properly before continuing to the next stage, as any mistakes or shortcuts will not be masked by the delicate flavour of the fish. You can use any fish you like, but something firm is best as a soft fish will tend to flake into the sauce quite quickly. I like to use steaks with large bones as they will impart a better flavour, but use fillets if you prefer. Ask your local fishmonger for fish that is fresh and works in a curry.

Heat the oil in a large non-stick saucepan. Add the whole spices and fry for 20 seconds. Add the onion and cook until golden. Meanwhile, using a blender, make a paste of the garlic and ginger with 50ml water. Add to the pan with the green chillies and cook until the oil comes out, around 4–5 minutes, stirring as it gets thicker.

Add the powdered spices and salt and stir to incorporate. Add the tomatoes and 100ml water and cook over a moderate-high heat until all the water has dried off. Then lower the heat and cook gently, covered, until the masala releases oil, around 6–8 minutes. Stir often as it gets thicker.

Add the cashew paste and stir fry for 2–3 minutes. Add 300ml water, bring to the boil and simmer, covered, for 15 minutes. Taste – the masala should be well rounded. Add more hot water for a creamy consistency. Taste and adjust the seasoning. Add the fish and coriander and cook until just done, around 3–4 minutes. Shake the pan rather than stirring, to avoid breaking up the fish.

Serves 4

2 tbsp coconut or vegetable oil
8 small green cardamom pods
5 cloves
2.5cm piece of cinnamon stick
1 medium–large onion, peeled and
    chopped
9g fresh ginger, peeled
7 large cloves of garlic, peeled
½ tsp red chilli powder, or to taste
½ tsp turmeric
1 rounded tbsp ground coriander
salt, to taste
2 medium tomatoes, quartered
1–2 green chillies, left whole
12 curry leaves
300ml coconut milk
400g raw prawns, peeled and deveined
½–¾ tsp tamarind paste, or to taste

Coastal Prawn Curry

This is a smooth coconut prawn curry with a beautiful peach colour and the essence of the Indian coast. Coconut oil adds the flavour of the coast and the strong smell disappears as it cooks. Lastly, add tamarind paste judiciously as I have found that different brands have different strengths – taste and add a little at a time. This curry is usually made with large prawns, but small ones work just as well and add a wonderful flavour to the gravy.

Heat the oil in a medium non-stick saucepan. Add the whole spices and cook until they are popping, then add the onion and cook until golden, around 8–10 minutes.

Meanwhile, using a blender, make a fine paste of the ginger and garlic with a little water. Add this to the pan and cook over a lowish heat for 2 minutes so that all the excess moisture dries off and you have fried the paste a little. Add the powdered spices, salt, tomatoes, green chillies and 50ml water and cook for 15 minutes. Taste the masala – it should have no harsh or raw elements to it.

Add the curry leaves, coconut milk and 100ml water, bring to the boil and simmer for 5 minutes for the flavours to blend. Add the prawns and cook for just 3 minutes, then take off the heat. Taste the curry and adjust the seasoning, then stir in the tamarind paste and serve.

Serves 2–4, or 6 as part of a meal

2 x 500–600g whole fish, such as sea
    bass or trout (ask your fishmonger to
    butterfly them)
1 tbsp vegetable oil

Green coconut chutney

12g coriander leaves and stalks
5 tsp lemon juice
salt, to taste
2 cloves of garlic, peeled
13g fresh ginger, peeled
1–3 long, thin green chillies, deseeded
100g fresh or frozen grated coconut
20 pistachio nuts
½ tsp cumin seeds
1 tsp vegetable oil
½ tsp brown mustard seeds

Baked Chutney-stuffed Fish

This is a simple fish dish that is easy enough to make for a family dinner but smart enough to serve to guests. It is a dish from the south, where green coconut chutney is used in cooking as opposed to being added as a condiment. I use sea bass because the flavour is delicate and neither the chutney nor the fish overpower each other. Buy this fish from a fishmonger or supermarket fish counter and ask them to butterfly the fish for you (my fishmonger removes the back bone and ribs, leaving just wonderful flesh which you can slice right through). I add pistachios, even though they are not a southern ingredient, as they bind the chutney together and make it creamy, which is sometimes necessary as the coconut we find here is not as moist as that in India. If you have a nut allergy, just leave them out.

Cut slashes along both sides of the fish at intervals of 2.5cm.

Using a blender, purée together all the ingredients for the chutney except the oil and mustard seeds. Heat the oil in a small saucepan, add the mustard seeds and when they start to pop, stir them into the chutney. Taste and slightly overseason.

Take out 2 tablespoons of the chutney and set aside. Add the tablespoon of vegetable oil to the remaining chutney and brush over the fish. Leave to marinate for 20 minutes, if you have time.

Preheat the oven to 180°C/350°F/gas mark 4. Spoon the reserved chutney into the fish cavities. Place the fish on a baking sheet or piece of foil and bake for 15–20 minutes or until cooked. Serve with some potatoes or a salad and a few lemon wedges.

Serves 4–5

400g medium raw prawns, peeled and
   deveined but with tail on
½ tsp turmeric
¼–½ tsp red chilli powder
salt, to taste
4 tbsp mustard oil
1 tsp nigella seeds
1–3 green chillies, left whole
1 small–medium onion, peeled and finely
   sliced
2 tsp garlic paste
2 tsp ginger paste
3–5 tsp English mustard, or to taste (I use
   around 4 tsp, see below)
1 tsp cornflour
130g fresh or frozen grated coconut
   (or 70g desiccated coconut soaked
   in water to cover)
handful of fresh coriander leaves and
   stalks, chopped

Coconut and Mustard Prawns

When I first tried these prawns, it was such a taste revelation. My mouth was buzzing with harmonious yet unusual flavours. This dish is not a mad concoction, as the name might suggest, but a show-case for the diversity of Indian food. Mustard in all its forms is an everyday ingredient in West Bengal and this dish shows how amazing this humble ingredient is. Usually the mustard in this dish would be a paste of fresh mustard seeds, but as I often find them a little bitter I have opted for proper English mustard that has exactly the same taste. Also, a true Bengali will enjoy a stronger taste of mustard than someone trying it out for the first time. So follow the guidelines and add mustard to taste. It is hard to imagine what this dish tastes like without trying it, so I urge you to give it a go as it is just amazing.

Marinate the prawns in a non-metallic bowl with the turmeric, red chilli powder and some salt for 30 minutes.

Heat the oil in a large non-stick karahi (see page 251) or saucepan until smoking, then take off the heat and cool for 15 seconds. Add the nigella seeds and cook until they sizzle. Add the green chillies and onion and cook until the onion is soft and just colouring, around 7–8 minutes. Add the garlic and ginger pastes and cook for 40 seconds.

Make a paste with the mustard, cornflour and a little water. Add the mustard paste and coconut and sauté for 5 minutes. Add 200ml water and cook for another 3–4 minutes. When it has reduced, add the prawns and cook, stirring, for 3 minutes or until they are ready. The gravy should be thick and clinging to the prawns. Stir in the coriander and serve.

Serves 4–6

5 tbsp mustard oil (preferably) or
    vegetable oil
4 green cardamom pods
4 cloves
3 small bay leaves
1 tsp panch phoran (see page 249)
1 small onion, peeled and finely chopped
2–3 green chillies, left whole but pricked
    with the tip of a knife
20g fresh ginger, peeled and pounded into
    a paste

2 large cloves of garlic, peeled and
    pounded into a paste
1 tbsp ground coriander
2 tsp ground cumin
½ tsp turmeric
⅛–¼ tsp red chilli powder
⅛ tsp paprika (optional, for colour)
salt, to taste
600g fish steaks (I like to use fresh
    sea bream, but see below), cleaned
    and cut into 2.5–4cm pieces

Bengali Fish Stew

This fish dish is the pride of most Bengali homes. It is homely, delicately spiced and often has vegetables added to it. The recipe changes from home to home, but fresh fish is always a requisite. The jhol or peach-coloured gravy is more like a flavoured stock and distinguishes a good Bengali cook from a bad one. I'm not sure if I would qualify as a good Bengali as my version is not traditional and I have omitted the vegetables that are usually fried and added in. Ideally use any firm, white-fleshed fish for these stews. You can use fillets but you will not get the flavour that you would with fish steaks. You can leave out the stage of frying the fish separately and can add it to the cooked bubbling broth, but it is better this way.

Heat 3½ tablespoons of the oil in a small non-stick saucepan until smoking, then remove from the heat for 20 seconds. Add the whole spices and panch phoran and fry over a low heat until they start to darken. Add the onion and cook until soft and translucent. Add the chillies, ginger and garlic pastes and cook over a low heat, stirring, for 1 minute. Stir in the powdered spices and salt, then add 400ml water. Bring to a boil, then simmer for 12–14 minutes. Set aside.

Meanwhile, heat the remaining oil in a large, deep sauté pan. Add the fish steaks and fry over a high heat for 1 minute on each side, then add to the gravy and simmer for 2 minutes or until done. Serve hot with rice.

Serves 1

1 medium mackerel, cleaned and de-boned
   if possible
$\frac{1}{4}$ tsp ginger paste
$\frac{1}{4}$ tsp garlic paste
salt, to taste
1 tbsp plus 1 tsp vegetable oil
2 tsp lemon juice
$\frac{1}{2}$ small onion, peeled and sliced
5 curry leaves
2 tsp Goan red spice paste (see page 13)
1 medium tomato, chopped
lemon wedges, to serve

Grilled Stuffed Mackerel

This is the perfect dish for those who love strong flavours, as the Goan red spice paste (which takes just a few minutes to make) is spicy and vinegary. The onions and tomatoes soften the paste and the curry leaves give it a fantastic flavour. I have written this recipe to serve one person as I always find there are never enough recipes for one, and the whole point of making pastes is to have quick and easy meals for small numbers. You can easily double or triple the quantities as necessary. In addition, you can make the stuffing mixture earlier in the day or even the night before, bringing it back to room temperature before baking. Mackerel is a good fish to use in this dish as it has a strong flavour that can hold its own with the masala.

Wash and dry the inside of the fish. Make deep slashes across both sides of the fish. Stir together the ginger and garlic pastes, salt, 1 teaspoon of the oil and the lemon juice and rub all over and into the slits of the fish. Place in a non-metallic dish, cover and marinate in the fridge for 30 minutes.

Heat the remaining oil in a small non-stick saucepan and fry the onion until golden brown. Add the curry leaves and masala paste and cook over a low–moderate heat for 3–4 minutes, stirring constantly. If you are concerned that the masala may burn, add a sprinkling of water to the pan. Add the tomato and salt and cook briskly for 6–8 minutes, stirring often. The tomatoes will completely break down and you will be left with a spicy, thick masala. Taste and adjust the seasoning.

Rub a little of this stuffing mixture on the flesh and inside the slits and stuff the rest into the cavity. Put the fish back in the fridge for another 20 minutes, if you have time.

Preheat the grill and cover the grill pan with kitchen foil. Place the fish on top and cook for 6–7 minutes on each side, turning carefully, until the fish is golden brown and cooked through. Serve with lemon wedges and plain rice.

3 tbsp vegetable oil
½ tsp brown mustard seeds
1 small onion, peeled and finely chopped
10g fresh ginger, peeled and finely
    chopped
2 large cloves of garlic, peeled and finely
    chopped
8 curry leaves
1 ½ tsp ground coriander
¼ tsp turmeric
¼ tsp red chilli powder, or to taste
¾ tsp garam masala
salt, to taste
2 small tomatoes, chopped
60g finely grated coconut, fresh or frozen
1 tsp lemon juice
30g salted roasted peanuts
300g salmon fillets, cut into 2.5cm cubes
handful of shredded crunchy lettuce
4 wheat tortillas

Keralan Salmon Wraps

The Keralan diet is replete with fish, so it is only to be expected that it transcends the curry and finds its way to other, exciting dishes. One of these is a deep-fried rice pancake that is stuffed with a spicy fish and coconut mixture. It is soft and spicy with a crisp exterior. Here I have simplified the idea, using the tortillas readily available in supermarkets and adding some lettuce and peanuts for crunch. The wraps are absolutely delicious, really quick and very easy – perfect for a mid-week meal for friends or family. The fish mixture also makes a great meal served with some vegetables.

Heat the oil in a medium non-stick saucepan and add the mustard seeds. Once they are popping, add the onion and fry until it is lightly coloured, around 7–8 minutes. Add the ginger, garlic and curry leaves and fry until the garlic starts to colour. Stir in the powdered spices and salt. Follow with the tomatoes, coconut and 200ml water. Bring to the boil, then cover and cook for 8–10 minutes or until the whole thing comes into a wonderful mass and everything tastes cooked. Add the lemon juice and peanuts and overseason slightly as the fish will absorb some of the salt.

Add the salmon and a splash of water if the pan is dry, then cover and cook over a low heat for 3–4 minutes or until the salmon is cooked through.

Place a long, thin bed of lettuce along the length of each tortilla. Top with a quarter of the salmon mixture and roll tightly. Halve through the centre and serve.

Chicken

4 tbsp vegetable oil
2 bay leaves
4 cloves
6 green cardamom pods
2 black cardamom pods
1 small–medium onion, peeled and sliced
15g fresh ginger, peeled
5 cloves of garlic, peeled
salt, to taste
¾ tsp red chilli powder (or paprika or
    Kashmiri chilli powder, for colour)
1 rounded tsp ground cumin
1 rounded tsp ground coriander
3 medium–large tomatoes, puréed
650g chicken joints or 4 large quarters,
    skinned

Kashmiri Chicken

This is a simple curry that uses lots of tomatoes and whole spices for its flavour. In Kashmir cooks traditionally use large pieces of chicken, and this dish would normally be made with a small quartered chicken, but you can use any joints you like for this easy-to-make dish. The flavours are simple, rustic and well rounded, and the curry is usually served with plain boiled rice.

Heat the oil in a large non-stick saucepan and add the whole spices; let them splutter for 15 seconds. Add the onion and cook until golden. Meanwhile, using a blender, make a fine paste of the ginger and garlic with a little water. Add to the pan and cook until the excess liquid has dried up and the paste has fried for 30 seconds. Add the salt, powdered spices and tomatoes. Cook, stirring occasionally, until oil is released from the masala, around 10–15 minutes.

Add 200ml water and bring to the boil, then taste and adjust the seasoning. Add the chicken pieces and cook, covered, until the chicken is cooked through, around 25 minutes. Take off the lid and add a splash of water from a recently boiled kettle if the gravy has reduced too much or, if necessary, burn off excess liquid over a high heat. Serve with rice.

Serves 6

20g fresh ginger, peeled
5 cloves of garlic, peeled
3 tbsp vegetable oil
1 medium onion, peeled and chopped
1–3 green chillies, left whole
800g chicken joints, skinned and bone in
2 heaped tbsp black masala (see page 12)
1 tsp garam masala
salt, to taste
2 medium tomatoes, puréed
¾–1 tsp tamarind paste
handful of fresh coriander leaves and
    stalks, chopped

Black Maharashtran-style Chicken

Maharashtra is the region to which Mumbai belongs. It was once a small fishing village and the Portuguese had aptly named it as such, *bom baim* or 'nice bay' which was then anglicized by the British to its former name of Bombay. Much of the region is coastal and the food is absolutely fantastic. Having said that, Pune, an inland city, is known as one of the region's best culinary spots and is home to black masala – the spice blend that gives this dish its character. This masala is a combination of roasted spices, sesame seeds and dried coconut (see page 12 for the recipe) and gives this dish a delicious nuttiness and background sweetness. A delightful and unusual dish that was inspired by black masala, this recipe has become one of my favourites ever since I first tried it.

Using a blender, make a fine paste of the ginger and garlic with a little water. Heat the oil in a large non-stick saucepan. Add the onion and cook until well browned, around 8–9 minutes. Add the ginger and garlic paste and the chillies and cook for 1 minute over a moderate heat, then add the chicken, black masala, garam masala and salt. Stir-fry for 5 minutes, then add the puréed tomatoes.

Cook, stirring, until the excess moisture in the pan has dried up. Add 250ml water to the pan, bring to the boil, then simmer, covered, for 20–25 minutes or until the chicken is cooked.

Stir in the tamarind paste, then taste and adjust the salt and tartness with more tamarind if necessary. Stir in the chopped coriander and serve.

Serves 6

20g fresh ginger, peeled and chopped
7 large cloves of garlic, peeled and chopped
3 tbsp vegetable oil
1 medium onion, peeled and chopped
salt, to taste
750g chicken pieces, skinned and jointed
2 medium–large tomatoes, puréed
12 large curry leaves
150–200ml coconut milk

Spice blend

2 tbsp white poppy seeds
1 heaped tbsp coriander seeds or ground
    coriander
1½ tsp cumin seeds
½ tsp turmeric
1 tsp garam masala
½–1 tsp red chilli powder
½ tsp black peppercorns
2 tsp fennel seeds

Keralan Chicken

Kerala is the spice garden of India and I will always associate the cooking with freshness. The spices are growing at their doorstep and are used so well that no single spice dominates – just flavourful harmony. Whilst we don't grow these spices in our backyard, we can easily find them not too far away or even via the computer screen. Look for large, minty-green fennel seeds for the best flavour. White poppy seeds will need to be bought from an Indian shop but are worth the trip – they are versatile, nutty and enrich any dish you add them to. Like many recipes, I have simplified this one a little; in case you want to go the whole way, finely slice a couple of shallots and fry until well browned, add the curry leaves at this stage, let them sizzle, then stir them into the finished dish for an extra layer of flavour and texture.

Using a blender, make a fine paste of the spice blend with the ginger, garlic and 100ml water.

Heat the vegetable oil in a large non-stick saucepan and fry the onion until brown, around 8–10 minutes. Stir in the spice paste and salt and cook over a moderate-high heat until completely reduced, then fry over a low heat for 1–2 minutes.

Add the chicken and lightly brown for 2 minutes, then add the curry leaves, tomatoes and 200ml water. Bring to the boil, cover and cook over a low heat, stirring occasionally, for 20 minutes. Uncover – there should still be lots of gravy in the pan; boil off over a high heat while tossing the chicken in the reducing gravy. When you have 1cm of gravy left, stir in the coconut milk and a good splash of water for a creamy curry, then bring back to a gentle boil. Check and adjust the seasoning and chilli. Serve with unleavened rice bread (see page 208), normal Indian breads or rice.

Serves 6–8

6 tbsp vegetable oil
1 medium–large onion, peeled, halved and
    finely sliced
salt, to taste
2 medium–large tomatoes, puréed
800g chicken, skinned and jointed
200g red lentils, rinsed well and soaked in
    water while you prepare and cook
4 small aubergines, halved lengthways
    (optional)
450g butternut squash, peeled and flesh
    cut into large chunks (optional)
1 tsp tamarind paste, or to taste
1 tsp garam masala
1 tsp sugar or jaggery (optional)
handful of fresh coriander, chopped

Paste

6 large cloves of garlic, peeled
10g fresh ginger, peeled
2 tsp cumin seeds
1 tbsp coriander seeds
2.5cm piece of cinnamon stick
¼ tsp fenugreek seeds, ground
½ tsp black mustard seeds
¼ tsp black peppercorns
1 tsp fennel seeds
½ tsp red chilli powder, or to taste

Chicken Dhansak

I generally shy away from dishes that have become so popular in the UK that their names are in the English lexicon. Dhansak would have been one of those dishes if I hadn't first tried it, by chance, in Mumbai. It was sublime: flavourful but not too spicy, slightly sweet but wholesome and served with brown rice; for me, it was perfect. It is an authentic Parsi dish that has made its way into this country for good reason. The gravy of a dhansak is made with lentils and often has pumpkin and aubergine in it as well as chicken or lamb, making it a complete, nutritious meal. But the vegetables are optional – you can leave them out or add others you have in your fridge. I have not yet tried this dish in any restaurants here, preferring not to tarnish the memory of my very first dhansak. Do try my version.

Using a blender, make a fine purée of the ingredients for the paste, adding a little water.

Heat the oil in a non-stick saucepan and fry the onion until well browned, around 8 minutes. Add the paste and salt and cook until all the moisture in the pan has dried up, then fry the paste for another 2–3 minutes over a low heat, stirring continuously. Add the tomatoes and a good splash of water, cover and cook for 10 minutes over a moderate–high heat or until the masala is cooked and the oil starts to bubble at the sides.

Add the chicken and brown for a few minutes. Drain the lentils from their soaking water and add to the pan with 800ml water. Bring to the boil, then simmer for 5 minutes. Add the aubergines, cover and cook over a low heat for 10 minutes, then add the squash, if using. Cover again and cook until the chicken and vegetables are tender, another 10 minutes or so. Give the pan an occasional stir to make sure the lentils are not settling at the bottom.

Add the tamarind paste to taste, the garam masala and sugar. Check the seasoning and, using the back of the spoon, crush some of the lentils to bind the gravy. Add a splash of recently boiled water from the kettle if it is too thick. Sprinkle over the coriander and serve.

Kerala

My experiences of Kerala are mainly of rest, relaxation and rejuvenation as I always

KERALA

combine my trips with a visit to one of the region's famous Ayurvedic spas. I do also manage to squeeze in languishing on the beaches, visiting historic sites, cruising slowly along the miles of the Keralan backwaters and, of course, sampling the food.

The Keralan culinary quilt is colourful and complex. It sometimes seems that anything goes in Kerala but one has only to look a little deeper to understand the influences. The Malayalis (as the Keralans call themselves) have an ancient heritage that is still evident in their local dances, martial arts and medicine. In more recent history, Kerala was an important trading port with the Middle East and many Jews, Muslims and Christians moved there and are still there today. The three main communities are the Hindus, Muslims and Christians, they all have different styles and collectively their cooking forms Malayali food.

The similarities between them are a testimony to Kerala's favourite ingredients – rice, fish and coconut – and the local spices of cinnamon, cloves, nutmeg, black peppercorns, mustard seeds and fenugreek seeds. Coconuts are used in all their stages, from tender to mature, for their water, flesh and oil, even the husks are used for fuel or to make rope. Rice is

the staple grain and is not only eaten plain and boiled, but is also made into dumplings, breads, noodles, pancakes and porridges. Fish include the estuarine Pearl Spot, the meaty seer fish, mussels, squid or prawns among others.

The different heritages and religions of the communities, however, ensure that there is life beyond the obvious local bounties. The Christians eat duck and beef, the Muslims also enjoy lamb and chicken, and the Hindus ensure that there are plenty of vegetable dishes to choose from. There is even a large Arab community, the Moplahs, who settled there over a century ago and who have introduced unusual dishes such as meat and wheat porridges and stuffed pot-roasted chicken. Bananas feature heavily, as there are around 300 local varieties. While still green, they are stir-fried with spices, they are also sliced and fried into banana chips (see page 45) and made into sweet cakes and fritters.

Keralan food is a melting pot of culinary cultures yet the dishes, like the people, somehow fit together, live in harmony and are all thoroughly Keralan. For some of the tastes of Kerala, try the Coconut Chicken Fry (see page 90), Keralan Sautéed Lamb (see page 129), Vegetables and Rice Noodles in a Coconut Broth (see page 154) and Unleavened Rice Bread (see page 208).

Serves 6

3 tbsp vegetable or coconut oil
5cm piece of cinnamon stick
6 green cardamom pods
6 cloves
1 large onion, peeled and thinly sliced
12 curry leaves
2–6 green chillies, whole
5cm piece of fresh ginger, peeled, halved
    lengthways and half sliced into long,
    fine strips (the other half kept for
    another use)
6 large cloves of garlic, peeled and thinly sliced
750g chicken joints, skinned
salt, to taste
2 tsp garam masala
180g fresh or frozen grated coconut
1–1½ tsp lemon juice
small handful of fresh coriander leaves
    and stalks chopped

Coconut Chicken Fry

Many Southern Indians eat a simple, home-cooked meal called fish fry or chicken fry. I have always loved the idea of that dish and imagined how it could be cooked. I learnt that it does require a succession of stir-frying ingredients one after the other, and the chicken is often fried first, kept aside and re-introduced later. I haven't fried the chicken in this dish but, apart from that, the ingredients used are quite traditional and are all thrown in and fried, so I have borrowed the name for this dish from the same region. It is really delicious and should appeal to the novice as well as the seasoned lover of Indian food.

Heat the oil in a non-stick saucepan. Add the whole spices and fry for 20 seconds. Add the onion and cook until golden brown. Add the curry leaves, chillies, ginger strips and garlic and cook for another 2–3 minutes over a low heat, or until the garlic is cooked.

Add the chicken and stir-fry over a moderate-high heat for 3–4 minutes. Both the chicken and the onions should have darkened. Add the salt, half the garam masala and enough water to cover the chicken by half. Bring to the boil, then cover and simmer for 15 minutes.

Uncover the pan, turn the heat up high and burn off the excess water, stirring often. Once there is almost no water left in the pan, add the remaining garam masala, the coconut and lemon juice. Stir-fry to mix, cover and cook until the chicken is tender, another few minutes or so, depending on joint size. Add the coriander, taste and adjust the seasoning and tartness, and serve. If you wish, scatter extra coconut over the top to garnish.

20g fresh ginger, peeled
6 large cloves of garlic, peeled
3 tbsp vegetable oil
1 medium onion, peeled and chopped
2 tsp ground coriander
salt, to taste
$\frac{1}{2}$–$\frac{3}{4}$ tsp red chilli powder
3 medium–large tomatoes, chopped
700g chicken joints, skinned
1 large red pepper, cored and cut into
        2.5cm squares
4 tbsp sour cream
1$\frac{1}{2}$ tsp garam masala

Chicken with Sour Cream and Red Pepper

This is not a common combination of ingredients, but it is one that works really well. It is one of those dishes that I have wanted to create for a while and finally got down to making. The resulting dish is delicious: creamy, tangy and slightly spicy, with the red pepper adding another level of flavour. The finished dish almost reminds me of a Hungarian dish with paprika and sour cream. This is an easy recipe to make and is great served with naan.

Using a blender, make a fine paste of the ginger and garlic with a splash of water.

Heat the oil in a large non-stick saucepan. Add the onion and cook until well browned. Add the ginger and garlic paste and cook until the water has dried off and the paste has fried for about 30 seconds. Stir in the ground coriander, salt and chilli powder. Follow with the tomatoes, cover and cook until they have softened and there is no moisture left in the pan. Uncover and stir-fry for about 5 minutes to finish cooking the masala; taste – there should be no harsh elements in the gravy.

Add the chicken and brown lightly for 2 minutes. Add 300ml water, bring to the boil, then cover and cook over a low heat for 15 minutes. Add the red pepper, cover once again, and cook for another 7–10 minutes or until the chicken is cooked through.

There should be quite a lot of liquid in the pan. Increase the heat to high and boil off the excess water while stirring the chicken (this will deepen the flavours of the dish) for about 3–4 minutes or until there is a 4cm depth of gravy in the pan. Add the sour cream and garam masala. Taste and adjust the seasoning and chilli. The gravy should be creamy but not too thick – if necessary, add a splash of hot water from a recently boiled kettle to loosen.

Chicken with Spinach

Serves 6

500g spinach, washed and any
    hard stalks removed
6 tbsp vegetable oil
3 black cardamom pods
2 bay leaves
5cm piece of cinnamon
2–5 green chillies, pricked with
    the tip of a knife
1 large onion, peeled and
    chopped

18g fresh ginger, peeled and
    roughly chopped
11 large cloves garlic, peeled
3 large tomatoes, quartered
800g chicken, skinned and cut
    into small joints
salt, to taste
2 tsp ground coriander
1½ tsp garam masala
4 tbsp natural yoghurt, stirred
    to remove lumps

We more or less grew up on this fantastic, classic Punjabi dish. It was one of the regulars at our table, but we didn't realize it might be there for nutrition rather than flavour. It is one of the dishes that you see on the menus of Indian restaurants, but this is the cream-free home-made version. It is a delicious one-pot meal that can stand alone on the table with just some Indian bread or rice and perhaps a bowl of yoghurt. I use baby spinach as it is easier to clean and has a wonderful, soft flavour, but large leaf spinach is what would be used traditionally.

Using a blender, make a purée of the spinach, adding a little water to help.

Heat the vegetable oil in a large non-stick saucepan. Add the whole spices and cook for 20 seconds. Add the green chillies and onion and cook until these are brown.

Meanwhile, using a blender, make a fine paste of the ginger, garlic and tomatoes. Add to the cooked onion along with the chicken, salt and remaining spices, stir well and cook for 15 minutes. Add the yoghurt and cook, stirring, until all the gravy has dried up. Taste and make sure the masala has cooked through.

Stir in the spinach and cook for 10–12 minutes over a moderate heat or until the chicken has cooked through. Partially cover the pan as the spinach will spit, and stir occasionally. Taste, adjust the seasoning and serve.

Red Goan Chicken

Serves 4–5

4 tbsp vegetable oil
1 large onion, peeled and sliced
4 tbsp Goan red spice paste (see page 13)
4 large tomatoes, chopped
salt, to taste
700g chicken joints, skinned

I love the Goan red spice paste (see page 13). It is spicy, chilli-like and vinegary and adds a real punch to anything it is added to. I have made my paste suitable for Western palates, but by no means is it mild or apologetic. I think this dish shows the flavours of the paste beautifully. The onion adds sweetness and the tomatoes balance out the flavours of the paste. If you like spicy dishes – and by this I don't mean red-hot – this is a great dish to try.

Heat the oil in a large non-stick saucepan. Add the onion and cook until browned, around 10 minutes. Add the spice paste and cook, stirring, for 2–3 minutes.

Add the tomatoes and salt, cover, and cook for 10 minutes or until the tomatoes have softened and reduced. Uncover the pan and toss the tomatoes in their own juices for another 6–8 minutes or until they have become a good shade darker.

Add the chicken and toss well in the pan for a few minutes. Add 250ml water, bring to the boil and cover. Cook over a low heat for 20 minutes if the joints are small, 25 minutes if large. Uncover, turn the heat up and boil off the excess moisture in the pan, tossing the chicken in the reducing gravy all the time. Doing this for 3–4 minutes will finish off the chicken, deepen the flavour and darken the colour. The gravy should be a dark red and quite thick. Serve with Indian bread.

Opposite: Red Goan Chicken

1kg chicken joints, skinned and pierced
      randomly with a fork
2–4 Indian or finger green chillies,
      whole or slit
large handful of coriander leaves and
      stalks, chopped
seeds from 1 fresh pomegranate,
      to garnish

Marinade

30g garlic cloves, peeled
30g fresh ginger, peeled
1½ tsp salt
1½ tbsp ground coriander
1½ tbsp dried pomegranate powder
2 tbsp vegetable oil
1½ tsp garam masala

Dried Pomegranate Chicken

This is an unusual dish that I have only ever eaten at home, but cannot believe others do not know about it or eat it regularly. It is the simplest of recipes but has lots of flavour. The pomegranate used in the dish is not the same variety we eat as a fruit. It is from a variety of pomegranate that is too sour to eat but perfect as a tangy souring agent in food. Milder than lemon juice and sweeter than tamarind, it imparts a subtle, flavoured sourness. The seeds are usually powdered or crushed and are wonderful added to many North Indian dishes. Once bought, it keeps really well in the larder.

Using a blender, make a paste of all the ingredients for the marinade with 150ml water. Place in a non-metallic bowl with the chicken, cover and marinate in a cool place for as long as possible (overnight is best). Bring back to room temperature before cooking.

Add the well-marinated chicken and the marinade to a large non-stick pan with the green chillies and 150ml water. Bring to the boil, then cover and cook over a low heat for 20–25 minutes. Give it the occasional stir and make sure there is always some water in the pan.

Uncover and turn the heat up. Reduce the excess water in the pan by cooking over a high heat while tossing the chicken in the reducing gravy. When completely reduced, add a good splash of water from a boiled kettle for a little gravy. Check for seasoning and tartness, you can add more dried pomegranate powder if it needs it. Stir in the fresh coriander and garnish with fresh pomegranate seeds.

Serves 2

2–3 tbsp vegetable oil
pinch of salt and freshly ground black
    pepper
$\frac{1}{4}$ tsp ground cumin
2 large slices of bread, crumbed and
    placed on a large plate
2 boneless chicken breasts, skinned and
    flattened with a meat mallet between
    two sheets of clingfilm to a thickness
    of 1cm
1 large egg, whisked
lemon wedges, to serve

Marinade

1 large clove of garlic, peeled
5g fresh ginger, peeled
$\frac{1}{2}$–$\frac{3}{4}$ small onion (depends how small),
    peeled
salt, to taste
$\frac{1}{4}$ tsp freshly ground black pepper
1$\frac{1}{2}$ tsp lemon juice
1 tbsp vegetable oil
$\frac{1}{2}$ tsp garam masala

The Raj's Chicken Cutlet

These pan-fried breaded chicken breasts are so obviously a dish fused from two different cuisines. However, it is a natural fusion and not one I have forced. During the reign of the Raj in Kolkata, there were times when Indian food was 'in', and times when it was 'out' and French food was de rigueur. But even when Indian food was eaten, it was often the British version of it that was made. This was one of those dishes and it has always appealed to me in concept, so I was very excited to learn that it is still eaten in modern Kolkata today and is known as an Anglo-Indian dish and revered for its history along with others of its kind. History aside, it is a quick, satisfying dinner from the past that still works amazingly well in the present.

Using a blender, whiz together the ingredients for the marinade until smooth. Taste and adjust the seasoning and lemon juice (it should be generous as it needs to flavour the chicken). Marinade the chicken in a non-metallic bowl for as long as possible, at least a few hours, in the fridge. Bring back to room temperature before cooking.

Heat the oil in a large non-stick frying pan. Mix the salt, pepper and cumin into the breadcrumbs. Dip the chicken breasts in the egg and then press both sides into the crumbs. Lay in the pan, turn the heat to moderate and fry for 1–2 minutes on each side, depending on the thickness. Serve hot with wedges of lemon.

Serves 6

15g fresh ginger, peeled and cut into
    large pieces
10 large cloves of garlic, peeled
4 small black cardamom pods
4 cloves
5cm piece of cinnamon stick
5 tbsp vegetable oil
1 bay leaf
1 medium onion, peeled and chopped

2 green chillies, whole but pricked with
    the tip of a knife
750g chicken joints, skinned
5 tsp ground coriander
2 tsp ground cumin
¼ tsp red chilli powder
½ tsp turmeric
1½ tsp garam masala
salt, to taste
3 medium tomatoes, cut into small wedges
large handful of fresh coriander, chopped

Punjabi Chicken Curry

This chicken curry is soul food for the Punjabis. It is neither sweet nor thick nor too spicy, but a harmony of our flavours that only complement rather than overpower the chicken. This is the chicken recipe that most of my friends have asked for. As with all Indian food, I must say that the tomatoes have to be the cheap variety, not plum or vine, and the onions must be well browned. As it is a Punjabi dish, it has an array of whole spices as well as a final hit of the aroma of garam masala added at the end. The fresh coriander should be added for flavour and not just for garnish. The secret to any well-cooked curry is the cooking of the masala – slowly and over time is the best way, so be a little patient as it is worth the effort. Eat with chapatti or roti or a pilaff.

Using a blender, make a fine paste of the ginger and garlic with a little water. Set aside.

Place the black cardamom pods in a mortar, give them a bash with the pestle, then remove the husks to leave only the seeds. Add the cloves and cinnamon and grind to a powder.

Heat the oil in a large non-stick frying pan. Add the bay leaf and onion and cook until brown, around 8–10 minutes. Add the green chillies and ginger and garlic paste and cook until just golden, around 2–4 minutes.

Add the chicken and brown gently, over a moderate heat. Stir in the spices and salt and give the pan a good stir. Add the tomatoes and enough water to come 2.5cm up the pan. Bring to the boil, then cover and cook over a low heat for 15 minutes.

Uncover the pan, increase the heat to high and brown the masala. This will add a lot of depth to the flavour. Toss and turn the chicken in the reducing paste. Once the water has reduced, lower the heat and continue for another few minutes – the masala should release some droplets of oil. Then add enough hot water to the pan to come more than halfway up the chicken joints, bring to the boil, stir in the fresh coriander and serve.

Serves 4–5

3 tbsp vegetable oil
5cm piece of cinnamon stick
1 medium onion, peeled and thinly sliced
2–4 thin green chillies, left whole or sliced
    lengthwise for more heat
5 large cloves of garlic, peeled
15g fresh ginger, peeled
700g chicken joints, skinned and bone-in
2–3 medium sized potatoes, peeled and
    cut into quarters

¾ tsp turmeric
1½ generous tsp ground coriander
¾ tsp cumin powder
½ tsp freshly ground black pepper
½ tsp garam masala
3 cloves, crushed to a powder
salt, to taste
2 handfuls frozen French beans, defrosted
¾–1 tsp tamarind paste, or to taste
large handful of fresh coriander leaves,
    chopped

Chicken and Potato Stew

This Goan-inspired stew has a lighter, thinner gravy than a curry but not less flavour. It is like any good chicken soup – full of goodness and the flavour of chicken, with tender pieces of meat falling off the all-important bones. I have added potatoes and beans to this recipe, but you can add any vegetables you have to hand, Indian or not. They will just add more goodness to your diet and add an extra element and flavour to the dish. I haven't added any cornflour to the gravy; instead, I mash a piece or two of the cooked potato and stir it back into the gravy to thicken. Serve with crusty bread for mopping up the delicious gravy. One caveat: please do not even think about making this dish with boneless cubes of chicken as the flavour is in the bones. If you really have no alternative, then replace some of the water with good-quality chicken stock. This stew is great for the kids, without the chillies, of course.

Heat the oil in a large non-stick saucepan, add the cinnamon and fry for 20 seconds. Add the onion and chillies and cook until the onion is well browned.

Meanwhile, using a blender, purée the garlic and ginger with a good splash of water and add to the pan. Cook until the moisture has dried up and the paste has had a chance to fry for 30 seconds. Add the chicken and brown lightly for 2 minutes, then add all the spices, salt, the potatoes and enough water to cover the chicken and potatoes. Bring to a boil, then reduce the heat to low–moderate, cover and cook until the chicken and potatoes are tender, around 20–25 minutes. Add the beans. Remove two chunks of potato, mash and stir back in to thicken the stew.

Stir in tamarind paste to taste as different brands have different strengths. Check and adjust the seasoning, then stir in the fresh coriander and serve.

Serves 4–6

25g fresh ginger, peeled and roughly
    chopped
12 large cloves of garlic, peeled
1 large tomato, chopped
150ml natural yoghurt
4 tbsp vegetable oil
1 tsp mustard seeds
1 tsp fennel seeds, ground to a powder
¾ tsp fenugreek seeds
½ tsp caraway seeds
1 tsp nigella seeds

1 small onion, peeled and chopped
1½ tsp ground cumin
2 tsp ground coriander
½ tsp turmeric
700g chicken, cut into small joints and
    skinned
3–6 fat green chillies, left whole but
    pricked with the tip of a knife
1 tsp garam masala
salt, to taste
lemon juice, to taste
small handful of fresh coriander leaves,
    chopped

Chicken with Pickling Spices

I sometimes wonder if I am writing recipes for Indians, non-Indians or for Indians who have lived mainly outside of India. I doubt you can group these recipes to suit one category over the other, regardless of how they look in the photos. Does everyone have to like the same dish? Probably not, but just as uninitiated palates will not appreciate the spicier dishes, Indians from India are not used to apologetic ones. This is the kind of dish that will be made for Indians, but I would definitely try it on other guests with seasoned palates. The dish is strong, spicy and evocative of the flavours of pickles, so if you like them, give this a go.

Using a blender, purée the ginger and garlic with 40ml water; set aside. Now purée the tomato with the yoghurt.

Heat the oil in a large non-stick saucepan and add the five different seeds. Once these start to pop, add the onion and cook until golden. Add the ginger and garlic paste, ground cumin, coriander and turmeric. Fry for 3–4 minutes over a gentle–moderate heat until the oil comes out at the sides, stirring often.

Add the chicken and brown lightly before stirring in the puréed tomatoes, chillies and 300ml water. Bring to the boil, then turn the heat down and simmer, covered, until the chicken is tender, around 20 minutes. Stir occasionally and check to see that there is always enough water in the pan; if not, add a splash from a recently boiled kettle.

Uncover the pan, turn up the heat and 'brown' the masala by reducing the water while you toss the chicken in the reducing gravy. Continue doing this until the oil is released by the masala, around 4 minutes (if necessary, add a good splash from the kettle). When done, stir in 100ml water to make the gravy and the garam masala and salt. Taste and adjust the seasoning. Add lemon juice if the yoghurt is not tart enough. Stir in the fresh coriander and serve.

Serves 6

4 tbsp vegetable oil
2 bay leaves
2 black cardamom pods
1 medium–large onion, peeled and
    chopped
20g fresh ginger, peeled
7 large cloves of garlic, peeled
800g chicken, skinned and jointed
salt, to taste
150ml natural yoghurt, stirred well

30g cashew nuts, blended into a paste
    with 2 tbsp water
¾ tsp red chilli powder
2 tsp ground coriander
2 small–medium tomatoes, puréed
1½ tsp garam masala powder
⅓ tsp green cardamom powder
1–3 tsp lemon juice (quantity depends on
    the tartness of the tomatoes and
    yoghurt so taste while adding)
4 hard-boiled eggs, shelled and sliced
handful of fresh coriander, chopped

Hyderabad Chicken Curry

This city has always been known for its elaborate feasts, excellent food, meticulous cooking and rich dishes intended for their now-abolished royalty. This dish is based upon one of those eaten in this city, except I have simplified it by leaving out some of the whole spices that would be added into the oil. I would also use deep-fried onions made into a paste, more cashews, cream and ghee for a typical dish. I pared it down to its basics, intending to build from here if necessary, but found the flavours were so rich and delicious in their own right that the rest was unnecessary. I mention this only for those die-hard cooks who want it to be more authentic, richer and more complex of flavour. This is an elaborate, regal dish that is fantastic for a dinner party.

Heat the oil in a large non-stick saucepan and fry the bay leaves and black cardamom pods for 20 seconds or so. Add the onion and cook until well-browned, around 8–10 minutes. Meanwhile, using a blender, make a fine paste of the ginger and garlic with a splash of water. Add to the pan and cook until the excess moisture has dried up and the paste has fried for 20 seconds.

Add the chicken to the pan and brown for a few minutes. Stir in the salt, yoghurt, cashew paste, chilli powder, ground coriander and puréed tomatoes. Cover and cook over a low heat, stirring occasionally, until the chicken is tender, around 25 minutes.

You shouldn't need to add any water to the pan, but if the dish seems dry, add a good splash from a recently boiled kettle and bring back to the boil. There should be enough for a light, creamy gravy. Stir in the garam masala, cardamom powder and lemon juice. To serve the dish, cover the surface with the sliced egg and sprinkle with the fresh coriander. Serve with Indian breads.

Meat

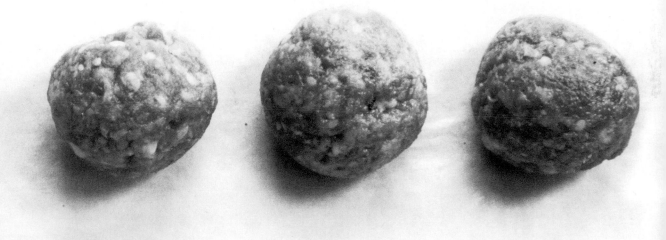

6 large cloves of garlic, peeled
6g fresh ginger, peeled
4 medium–large tomatoes, skinned if
    possible
250ml natural yoghurt
4 tbsp vegetable oil
3 black cardamom pods
3 cloves
5cm piece of cinnamon stick
2 green cardamom pods
10 black peppercorns
2 bay leaves
salt, to taste
$\frac{1}{2}$–$\frac{3}{4}$ tsp red chilli powder
600g cubed lamb, bone in (use leg or
    shoulder of lamb; see page 10)

Lahori Lamb

This dish came my way via an old friend of my father. Having visited Lahore recently, he fell in love with this dish and asked the cook to teach him how to make it. He brought it back to his house, it soon migrated to my father's house and both men were really keen I try it. To be honest, I wasn't sure what all the fuss was about, then we made it and I understood – it just worked. Whilst I have hardly changed the ingredients going into the dish, aside from halving the quantity of oil, I have completely changed the cooking method, from being a two-pot cooking process to just one. The flavour has not suffered and is still deep and harmonious.

Using a blender, make a fine paste of the garlic and ginger, adding a little water to help. Set aside. Using the same blender jug, purée the tomatoes with the yoghurt.

Heat the oil in a large non-stick pan and add the whole spices and bay leaves. Let them sizzle for 10 seconds, then add the ginger and garlic paste. Cook, stirring, over a moderate heat for 1–2 minutes or until the water has dried off and the paste has had a chance to fry for 20 seconds. Add the salt and red chilli powder, give the pot a good stir, then add the yoghurt and tomato mixture. Bring to the boil, then add the lamb. Bring back to the boil and cook over a low heat until the lamb is tender, around 35–40 minutes.

Take off the lid, turn up the heat and toss and turn the meat in the thickening gravy. This is an important step and will add depth to the curry. If there is little gravy in the pan, it is worth adding a good splash of water at this stage. Reduce to a depth of just 1cm of gravy in the pan. Once done, add enough water from a recently boiled kettle to make a creamy gravy.

Serves 6

4 tbsp vegetable oil
3 black cardamom pods
1 medium onion, peeled and chopped
10g fresh ginger, peeled
6 cloves of garlic, peeled
1 tbsp ground coriander
$\frac{1}{4}$–$\frac{1}{2}$ tsp red chilli powder
$1\frac{1}{2}$ tsp ground cumin
$1\frac{1}{2}$ tsp garam masala
1 tsp freshly ground black pepper

salt, to taste
450g lamb mince
150ml lamb or chicken stock
2 tbsp Worcestershire sauce
2 medium tomatoes, chopped
50g butter
250ml milk (for a richer dish, substitute
    cream for some of the milk)
700g potatoes, boiled whole, skinned
    and mashed
3 handfuls of frozen peas

Indian Shepherd's Pie

I had been meaning to write a recipe for an Indian shepherd's pie for a long time, so when I decided to include some typical Anglo-Indian recipes from the Raj in this book, I knew this was the time to do so. This recipe is inspired by the dishes of Kolkata – this was the capital of India and the British government was based there. Whilst I am not sure if shepherd's pie was ever one of their dishes, they ate many that were similar. Leftover meats were often minced and spiced and either rolled into pancakes and deep-fried or encased in mashed potato, then crumbed and fried. I used these flavours as guidelines and got creative. By the time I had finished, the dish had become more Indian and less Anglo, but still really delicious.

Heat the oil in a large non-stick saucepan, add the cardamom pods and cook for 30 seconds. Add the onion and cook until golden brown. Meanwhile, using a blender, make a fine paste of the ginger and garlic, adding a good splash of water. Add to the pan with all the spices and salt. Cook for 1 minute, then add the lamb; brown over a moderate heat for 6 minutes.

Add the stock, Worcestershire sauce and tomatoes. Bring to the boil, then cover and simmer for 15 minutes. Allow to cool and remove the black cardamom pods. There should be a little liquid still left in the pan.

Preheat the oven to 180°C/350°F/gas mark 4.

Heat the butter and milk (with the cream, if using) in a pan until hot, season well and stir in the mashed potatoes. Stir lightly and quickly to incorporate, then check and adjust the seasoning and remove from the heat.

Stir the peas into the lamb and place in an ovenproof dish. Top with the potatoes. Bake in the oven for 30 minutes or until hot and bubbling. Let it stand for 5 minutes before serving.

Serves 6

3–4 tbsp vegetable oil
7 black peppercorns
2 black cardamom pods
5 green cardamom pods
3 cloves
5cm piece of cinnamon stick
1 blade of mace
1 large onion, peeled and finely sliced
750g lamb or mutton, bone in, cut into
    3cm cubes (ideally leg of lamb or
    shoulder of mutton; see page 10)

6 large cloves of garlic, peeled
12g fresh ginger, peeled and halved
2 tsp ground coriander
2 tsp ground cumin
1 tsp red chilli powder
2 tsp fennel seeds, powdered
1½ tsp garam masala
salt, to taste
2 medium–large tomatoes, puréed
3 tbsp natural yoghurt, stirred well to break
    up any lumps
handful of fresh coriander leaves and
    stalks, chopped

My Roganjosh

We all know roganjosh and we all have certain expectations of it. Probably none of them is the original, which hails from Kashmir and has picked up chefs' influences along the way. I'm not sure what you will expect from this dish as your experience of roganjosh will vary depending on where you ate it and who cooked it for you; this one is a hearty lamb curry. It is the kind of curry that may initially seem complicated as the list of ingredients is fairly lengthy, but I have tried to keep chopping to a minimum. If you don't have the whole spices to hand, the dish can still be made by adding a little more garam masala at the end. You might not get the same depth of flavour that you would using whole spices, but you will still have a fantastic meal.

Heat the oil in a large non-stick saucepan. Add the whole spices and fry until sizzling. Add the onion and cook until golden, around 8–10 minutes. Add the lamb and stir until coloured all over, about 3 minutes.

Meanwhile, using a blender, make a fine paste of the garlic and ginger with a good splash of water. Add to the pan, lower the heat and cook for about 2 minutes, stirring, or until you can smell the cooked garlic. Stir in the powdered spices and salt and stir for 40 seconds. Stir in the tomatoes, turn the heat up a little and cook until the oil leaves the masala, around 15 minutes, stirring occasionally. You may need to add a splash of water from a recently boiled kettle if it all dries up too quickly.

Add enough water to come halfway up the meat and bring to the boil, then turn the heat right down and simmer until the meat is tender, around 35–45 minutes, depending on the joints. By this time the gravy should be creamy. Stir in the yoghurt to mix well, once it comes back to the boil. Remove from the heat, stir in the fresh coriander and serve.

Serves 4–6

400g lamb mince, extra finely minced (ask your butcher to mince it three times)
2 large slices of white bread, crusts removed and crumbed
1 egg, whisked
salt, to taste, and freshly ground black pepper
1½ tsp garam masala
2 tsp ground cumin
2 tbsp vegetable oil
1 small–medium onion, peeled and finely chopped
15g fresh ginger, peeled and quartered
7 large cloves of garlic, peeled
2–6 thin green chillies, deseeded if preferred
350ml coconut milk
1½ tsp ground coriander
40g fresh coriander leaves and stalks
1 tsp tamarind paste, or to taste

Green Meatball Curry

This curry has been inspired by the meatball stews of Goa. It is a beautiful dish and the flavours are deep and well rounded. It is perfect for an easy dinner and great for children (without the chillies) as they can help form the meatballs, as I did when young. The curry itself only requires the chopping of an onion and a hand blender. Serve it with basmati rice, bread, rice noodles or even mashed potatoes – anything to soak up the delicious gravy.

Mix the mince with the breadcrumbs, egg, ½ teaspoon salt and a good grinding of pepper, ½ teaspoon garam masala, 1 teaspoon ground cumin and 1 teaspoon of the oil. Form into small meatballs and set aside.

Heat the remaining oil in a large non-stick saucepan. Add the onion and fry until brown. Meanwhile, using a blender, make a paste of the ginger, garlic and chillies with 100ml of the coconut milk. Add this to the pan with the remaining spices and salt. Cook over a moderate heat for 8–10 minutes or until the masala releases oil and has no harsh elements when tasted.

Purée the fresh coriander with the remaining coconut milk and add to the cooked masala with 400ml water. Bring to the boil and cook for 8–10 minutes. Taste the seasoning and adjust, adding as much tamarind paste as you like for sourness. Add all the meatballs and bring back to the boil, then cook over a low heat for 20 minutes or until the lamb is tender.

15g fresh ginger, peeled
4 large cloves of garlic, peeled
4 large tomatoes, chopped
2–3 green chillies, slit and deseeded
4 tbsp natural yoghurt, stirred to break up
    any lumps
1½ tbsp ground coriander
1½ tsp caraway seeds
10 small green cardamom pods, seeds
    removed and ground
salt, to taste
4 tbsp vegetable oil
750g lamb, bone in, cut into 5cm cubes
    (ideally use leg or shoulder; see page 10)
1 medium–large onion, peeled and
    chopped
good handful of fresh coriander, chopped

Sindhi Lamb Curry

This dish was given to me by the mother of a friend. She is Sindhi, so although this may seem like another traditional North Indian curry, it isn't. It has the depth of flavour you would expect, but isn't as spicy. The trick is to brown the meat over a low heat without adding any water for as long as possible. The flavour really develops as you do this. If you don't have the time, add a splash of water with the tomatoes and leave the lamb to cook until tender.

Using a blender, make a paste of the ginger and garlic with a splash of water. Mix with the tomatoes, green chillies, yoghurt, ground coriander, caraway seeds, ground cardamom, salt and 1 tablespoon of the vegetable oil. Place in a non-metallic bowl and add the lamb. Stir, cover and leave to marinate in the fridge for as long as possible. Bring back to room temperature before cooking.

Heat the remaining oil in a large non-stick saucepan, add the onion and fry until golden. Add the lamb and marinade, and bring to the boil. Cover and cook over a low heat until the lamb is cooked through, around 30 minutes, stirring every now and again.

Uncover and continue cooking the meat, adding no water, until the lamb has browned a little and the masala releases oil onto the surface, around 15 minutes. Stir in the fresh coriander and serve.

Serves 4

1 tsp cumin seeds
1 tsp coriander seeds
5 black peppercorns
2 green cardamom pods
2 cloves
2.5cm piece of cinnamon stick
13g fresh ginger, peeled and roughly cut
7 large cloves of garlic, peeled
2–4 fresh large red chillies (quantity
  depends on their heat and your
  enjoyment of it)

3 tbsp good-quality white wine vinegar
400g pork shoulder with some fat on it,
  cut into 2.5cm cubes
50g belly of pork, cut into 2.5cm cubes
4 tbsp plus 1 tsp vegetable oil
1 small onion, peeled and finely chopped
salt, to taste
$3/4$ tsp mustard seeds
handful of cashew nuts

Pork Vindaloo

The Portuguese were such lovers of pork that they stored it in barrels with ginger, garlic and lots of white wine vinegar to preserve it on long sea journeys. I see this as the beginning of the vindaloo. Even now, Goans add a cupful of vinegar to help preserve it for a week or more. It is supposed to be a spicy, sour dish, but many restaurants don't use an authentic recipe. My version is more balanced, with a moderate amount of chilli and vinegar, but both these elements can be increased at the end if you wish. I have added mustard seeds and cashew nuts for added nutty flavour and a burst of texture. I was given a tip by a Goan that the only way to cook this dish is in its own juices, adding no water to the pan. The way he does it (I have tried it and it works) is to cover the pan with a plate that is slightly concave, fill the indent with cold water, turn the heat down and refresh the water in the plate every 6 minutes or so. It keeps the water and steam in the pan. For an easier ride, add only a small splash of water once the pork's own natural juices have dried up and keep adding splashes from a boiled kettle when necessary.

Using a spice grinder, grind the whole spices to a fine powder. Using a blender, make a fine paste of the ginger, garlic, chillies and vinegar. Place the pork in a non-metallic dish along with the spices and salt, cover and marinate for a couple of hours, if you have time. Bring back to room temperature before cooking.

Heat 4 tablespoons of the oil in a medium, deep non-stick saucepan. Add the onion and fry until golden brown. Add the pork and marinade and brown gently over a moderate heat for 6–7 minutes. Turn the heat to low, cover and cook until the pork is done, around 40 minutes (or see above). Stir occasionally and add a splash of water whenever the pan looks like it is running dry. The end result should be a wonderful medium–thick gravy.

Heat the remaining oil in a small saucepan, add the mustard seeds and once they start to pop, add the cashew nuts and cook until golden. Pour them over the vindaloo and serve.

You can also serve the hot pork vindaloo in wheat tortillas with some lettuce and sour cream.

Serves 6

4–8 fat mild red chillies, slit or halved
6 large cloves of garlic, peeled
4 tbsp vegetable oil
6 small lamb shanks, French-trimmed
   (see below)
5cm piece of cinnamon stick
1 blade of mace
10 small green cardamom pods
1 medium–large onion, peeled and
   chopped

12g fresh ginger, peeled and sliced into
   julienne strips
200ml natural yoghurt
1 tbsp white poppy seeds, made into a
   paste with a little water using a pestle
   and mortar
3 tbsp desiccated coconut
salt, to taste
2 ½ tbsp finely ground almonds
1 tsp garam masala
handful of fresh coriander leaves and
   stalks, chopped

Red Lamb Shank Korma

This dish is reminiscent of the rich Mogul dishes served in Lucknow to royalty of old. A korma is usually milder and smoother than a deep, rich curry, but this dish is a combination of both. I have added red chillies and they add a beautiful, rounded flavour and, yes, a little kick, but using mild chillies ensures it is just a small one. Lamb shanks are actually very easy to cook as long as you have time and a big pot, and the rewards in terms of flavour are unsurpassable. Buy small ones for individual portions and ask the butcher to French-trim them (i.e. clean the meat from the bones) for you for a cleaner presentation.

Using a blender, make a paste of the chillies and garlic, adding a splash of water.

Heat the oil in a large pan and brown the lamb shanks all over. Remove them and set aside. Add the whole spices to the pan and cook for 30 seconds. Add the onion and cook until golden brown, around 7–8 minutes. Stir in the paste and ginger and cook for 1–2 minutes or until the excess moisture has dried up and the paste has fried. Return the lamb to the pan with any juices that have spilled onto the plate.

Whisk together the yoghurt, poppy seed paste, coconut and salt and add to the pan. Pour in enough water to come three-quarters of the way up the shanks. Bring to a boil and then cook, covered, over a low heat until the lamb is tender, about 1 hour. Give the pot a good stir every now and then and add a good splash of water from a recently boiled kettle, if necessary.

When the meat is cooked and tender, add the ground almonds and garam masala. The gravy should be creamy, so add a splash of water from the kettle to loosen or boil away the excess liquid over a high heat until the gravy has the right consistency. Taste and adjust seasoning and serve garnished with the coriander.

You can also cook this dish in the oven. Once you have cooked the onion, ginger and garlic and browned the lamb shanks, place everything in a large baking dish with a lid and cook for 1½–2 hours at 180°C/350°F/gas mark 4.

Serves 4–5

7 cloves of garlic, peeled
12g fresh ginger, peeled, half sliced into
    long julienne strips (the rest is for
    the paste)
½–¾ tsp red chilli powder
1½ tsp ground coriander
500g boneless lamb, cut into 2cm cubes
3 tbsp coconut oil or vegetable oil
3 cloves
1 piece of cinnamon stick

3 green cardamom pods
½ tsp mustard seeds
15 curry leaves
2–4 green chillies
1 small–medium onion, peeled and
    chopped
1 medium–large tomato, chopped
120g fresh or frozen grated coconut
¾ tsp garam masala
1 rounded tsp fennel seeds, powdered
salt, to taste, and ¼ tsp freshly ground
    black pepper

Keralan Sautéed Lamb with Coconut

This is a delicious curry, full of spices and coconut, both of which befit a Keralan dish. It is a dry dish, made with fresh coconut when I want to go that extra mile, but more often than not I use the frozen grated coconut now available in Asian stores and some supermarkets instead. I highly recommend buying a packet; it can be used in sweet and savoury dishes and lasts forever. Coconut oil is the oil of choice here and does add an extra flavour, but the dish works just as well without, so don't be put off if you don't have any. Serve with a roti, naan or rice bread dipped in coconut milk, garnished with fried curry leaves and more coconut.

Using a blender, make a paste of the garlic and reserved ginger with a small splash of water. Place in a non-metallic bowl with the red chilli powder and ground coriander, add the lamb and mix well to coat. Leave to marinate in a cool place for a few hours.

Heat the oil in a large non-stick saucepan. Add the whole spices and mustard seeds and fry for 20 seconds or until they are spluttering. Stir in the ginger strips and cook for 10 seconds. Add the curry leaves, green chillies and onion and cook until they are soft and golden.

Add the lamb and its marinade, cover and cook over a low heat for 15–20 minutes or until the lamb is just tender. You may need to add the occasional small splash of water from a recently boiled kettle if the masala looks ready to catch the base of the pan. Add the tomato and coconut and stir-fry until the tomatoes have softened, around 5 minutes. Stir in the garam masala and fennel seed powder, taste and adjust the seasoning. The dish should be moist but without a gravy, so dry off any extra liquid over a high heat and serve.

4 tbsp vegetable oil
2 black cardamom pods
2.5cm piece of cinnamon stick
10 black peppercorns
3 cloves
2 bay leaves
1 medium onion, peeled and sliced
2–4 green chillies, left whole
6 lamb chops, fat removed
5 large cloves of garlic, peeled and made
    into a paste with a little water
12g fresh ginger, peeled and cut into
    julienne strips
2 largish tomatoes, cut into thin wedges
salt, to taste
1 tsp ground cumin
¾ tsp dried pomegranate powder
½ tsp garam masala
2 tsp ground coriander
handful of fresh coriander leaves and
    stalks, chopped

Punjabi Lamb Chops

A delicious, rustic dish which is the essence of what the region stands for – full-flavoured, full-bodied food, no fuss and no pomp. The whole spices add a depth of flavour and yet there is a freshness from cooking the remaining flavours briefly and in chunks. Despite the lengthy list of ingredients, it is a really quick recipe but not a mild one, so if you are still discovering the bold flavours of the region this is one you might come back to later. As with most Indian dishes, plum tomatoes add too much sweetness, so stick to the cheaper family pack of tomatoes.

Heat the oil in a large non-stick saucepan. Add the whole spices and bay leaves and allow them to sizzle for 20 seconds. Add the onion and cook until well browned. Add the green chillies and the lamb chops and brown them on both sides.

Add the garlic paste, ginger, tomatoes, salt, cumin and dried pomegranate powder and stir-fry for 5 minutes. Add 100ml water, bring to the boil, cover and cook over a moderate heat for 6–8 minutes. There should be just enough water in the pan for a little gravy; if not, add a splash of water from a recently boiled kettle. If the gravy seems too watery, reduce over a high heat for a few minutes.

Taste and adjust seasoning and stir in the garam masala and ground coriander. Cook for another minute and serve garnished with fresh coriander.

Punjab

Punjabis are a proud, exuberant, warm and fun-loving people.

They have a zest for life that encompasses love, music, dancing, parties and, most of all, food. They consider themselves lucky as the Punjab is the most fertile region in India. Wheat, vegetables, lentils and sugar cane are grown, there is land for grazing and rivers for fish. Whilst most Indian restaurants in the West are known for their northern dishes, few capture the true range and flavours found in Punjabi homes. The dishes are all flavoured and spiced differently depending on what you are cooking; every vegetable, grain and meat is treated individually, there is no generic 'curry'. It is the artistry of the cook to use the same colourful palette of spices to create dishes that are distinct. The main ones used in this region are those collectively known as garam masala – cloves, cinnamon, black cardamom pods, black pepper, bay leaves, coriander seeds and mace.

My father tells stories of going to the river with his brothers to catch fish, which would end up either fried or simmered in a pot of bubbling tomato gravy, or buying chicken and cooking it together, but by the time dinner was served, most of it had been eaten straight from the pan as they tasted and discussed which spices

to add. Bread was wholemeal and cooked in the communal neighbourhood tandoors for that special charcoal flavour. Milk is still plentiful and each home turns it into yoghurt, butter, cream and the king of dairy products – paneer. This is one of Punjab's culinary contributions to the world: a fresh, white cheese originally made with buffalo milk and as creamy and soft as the best mozzarella. It is perhaps the only cheese still made at home (see page 13). Life was simple, but the food was good and that was enough.

Desserts are reflective of the people – hearty and homely – and made with the wholesome fruits of the land. They are creamy, sweet and comforting. I love them and eaten in moderation, as they are meant to be, I feel that I am nourishing my body while enjoying my pudding.

I don't think Punjab has changed much over the years. People are wealthier, refrigeration has arrived, ingredients are more accessible and the West has crept in with the satellite, but the people still prefer to cook with the seasons and remain true to the region. For a taste of the Punjab, try the Battered Amritsari Sole (see page 60), Punjabi Chicken Curry (see page 103), Punjabi Lamb Chops (see page 130) or Roti (see page 211).

Serves 4–6

15g fresh ginger, peeled
6 large cloves of garlic, peeled
4 tbsp vegetable oil
1 medium onion, peeled and chopped
12 curry leaves
600g lamb, bone-in, or 450g lamb rump,
    fat trimmed and cut into 4cm cubes
    (see page 10)
3 tsp ground coriander
½ tsp turmeric
2 tsp ground cumin
1 tsp freshly ground black pepper
1¾ tsp garam masala
salt, to taste
2 medium tomatoes, chopped
¼ tsp tamarind paste, or to taste

Madras Pepper Lamb

A simple, delicious recipe from the state of Tamil Nadu. This is a deep, well-rounded lamb dish with accents of the curry leaves and fresh black pepper that show it to be from that region. It is not a curry as it is not a saucy dish, but one where the gravy clings to the tender meat. Use good-quality lamb – I sometimes use boneless rump, trimming the fat, browning cubes of meat and adding them to the cooked gravy (they only need the gentlest 5 minutes of cooking to be tender and pink), but generally I use lamb from the shoulder or leg with the bone in and allow it to cook until falling off the bone. Serve with naan or Indian bread.

Using a blender, make a fine paste of the ginger and garlic with a splash of water.

Heat the oil in a medium non-stick saucepan. Add the onion and fry until golden. Add the curry leaves and paste and cook for 1 minute. Add the lamb and brown over a moderate heat, stirring continuously.

Add all the spices, salt and tomatoes, and give the pan a good stir. Add enough water to come halfway up the lamb. Bring to a gentle simmer, cover and cook until done, around 20–30 minutes. (If using lamb rump, brown for 5 minutes over a gentle heat and add to the cooked gravy.)

Stir in the tamarind paste, taste and adjust the seasoning, then serve.

Serves 6–8

3 tbsp vegetable oil
600g lamb rump, cut into 2.5cm pieces
    with the fat removed
1 tsp mustard seeds
1 large onion, peeled and finely chopped
20g fresh ginger, peeled
5 large cloves of garlic, peeled
salt, to taste
1 tsp sugar
1 tbsp ground coriander

1 tbsp ground cumin
½ tsp turmeric
¼–½ tsp red chilli powder, or to taste
3 medium tomatoes, puréed
400ml can coconut milk
1–2 tsp lemon juice. or to taste
1 small sweet potato, peeled and cut into
    large chunks
250g can chickpeas, drained and rinsed
1¼ tsp garam masala
handful of fresh coriander, chopped

Fenugreek dumplings

100g chapatti flour or wholemeal flour
45g gram flour
2 tbsp dried fenugreek leaves or 4 tbsp
    fresh leaves, chopped
1½ tsp grated fresh ginger
¾ tsp salt
1½ tsp sugar
¼ tsp turmeric
1 tbsp lemon juice
2 tbsp oil
⅓ tsp baking powder

Gujarati Lamb and Dumpling Stew

This is a dish inspired by Gujarati flavours. Whilst most Hindu Gujaratis are vegetarian, not all Gujarati food is. Traditionally, many Gujaratis who lived by the sea included fish in their diet. In Surat, Gujarat's second largest city, fish was eaten on certain auspicious days to ensure a bountiful year, and Muslim Gujaratis have a wonderful cuisine, full of meat curries, biryanis and kebabs. This is a hearty, autumnal one-pot meal with tender pieces of lamb nestling between light and soft dumplings, chunks of sweet potato and little earthy bites of chickpea. The spices are moderate, with a touch of sweetness and lots of textures. You can change the vegetables or beans to your own taste.

Heat the oil in a large non-stick saucepan, add the lamb and brown lightly on all sides. Take out and keep to one side. Add the mustard seeds and when they start to pop, add the onion and fry until brown.

Meanwhile, using a blender, make a paste of the ginger and garlic with a good splash of water. Add this to the onion and cook until reduced and gently colouring, around 3 minutes. Add the salt, sugar, ground coriander, cumin, turmeric and chilli powder and cook over a low heat for 20 seconds.

Add the tomatoes and 100ml water and cook gently until completely reduced, then fry the paste for 5–6 minutes or until the oil comes out. It should be dark and smooth to taste.

Meanwhile mix all the ingredients for the dumplings, adding 2 tablespoons of water slowly, and if necessary, to make a semi-soft dough. Make into 3 sausage shapes and pinch off 6 pieces from each sausage. Roll each into a small, smooth ball and squeeze in the palm of your hand to make small dumplings. They expand while cooking.

Add the coconut milk, lemon juice and 200ml water to the saucepan. Bring to a gentle boil, then simmer for 5 minutes. Add the sweet potato and bring back to the boil. Add the dumplings after another 6 minutes and cook, covered, for 6 minutes.

Add the lamb and chickpeas, cover and cook for 4–6 minutes or tender. Stir in the garam masala and fresh coriander and serve.

Serves 4

1½ tbsp ghee or vegetable oil
600g leg of lamb, cut into 4cm cubes,
    bone in (see page 10)
1 tbsp fennel seeds, powdered
2 tsp ground ginger
2 black cardamom pods
1 bay leaf
6 cloves
10cm piece of cinnamon stick
7 green cardamom pods, pricked with
    the tip of a knife
salt, to taste
700ml milk
1 tsp freshly ground black pepper
½ tsp garam masala
½ tsp sugar

Kashmiri Lamb cooked in Milk

This is a delicate dish where lamb is cooked in spiced stock, then added to creamy, reduced milk. In Kashmir, extra lamb bones are sometimes added to the cooking meat for additional flavour, but a little lamb stock also does the trick. As befits a Hindu Kashmiri dish, there are no onions or garlic – all the flavour comes from the spices. There is no chilli in this dish as that too would change the flavour and take away from the dish's subtlety, but there is a good amount of black pepper stirred in at the end for added kick. Another wonderful addition would be a sprinkling of saffron strands on top of the finished dish, as they will ooze their wonderful colour and flavour into the calm milky gravy. Serve with Kashmiri rice or plain boiled rice. If you don't have ground ginger, add a few slices of fresh ginger instead.

Heat the oil in a large saucepan, add the lamb and sear on all sides. Add 750ml water and the spices and salt. Bring to the boil, cover and simmer over a low heat until the lamb is tender, around 30 minutes. Strain the lamb and spices and reduce the meat stock until there is just 100ml of liquid left. Discard the whole spices.

Meanwhile, pour the milk into another saucepan. Cook over a low heat, stirring often, until it is reduced to half its volume, around 25 minutes. Make sure that you scrape the base of the pan to stop the milk catching and burning.

Add the cooked lamb, reduced stock, black pepper, garam masala and sugar and bring slowly back to the boil. Serve with rice.

14g fresh ginger, peeled
5 large cloves of garlic, peeled
4 tbsp vegetable oil
1 medium onion, peeled and chopped
2 tsp white poppy seeds
5 tbsp desiccated coconut
400g boneless lamb, cut into 2.5cm cubes
salt, to taste
½ tsp red chilli powder, or to taste
¾ tsp garam masala
3 rounded tsp black masala powder, or to
    taste (see page 12)
6 tbsp coconut milk
½–¾ tsp tamarind paste, or to taste

Maharashtran Lamb Curry

This is a delicious creamy lamb curry from the state of Maharashtra, on the western coast of India. The main star here is the sweet black masala of the roasted spices – this, with the coconut, ensures a wonderful nutty flavour to go with the lamb, contrasted with a good amount of tamarind paste. You can buy black masala (also known as Goda masala), but it is never as fresh as home-made.

Using a blender, make a smooth paste of the ginger and garlic with a little water.

Heat the oil in a non-stick saucepan, add the onion and cook until golden. Remove half and reserve. Add the poppy seeds and desiccated coconut to the pan and continue cooking until golden. Scrape into a blender and blend to a fine paste, adding a little water to help, then set aside.

Spoon the reserved onions back into the pan, reheat and add the ginger and garlic paste. Cook until golden, around 2–3 minutes. Add the lamb and brown evenly, stirring often, around 4 minutes. Stir in the salt and spices and cook for 1 minute, stirring constantly.

Add the coconut milk, tamarind paste and the onion and poppy seed paste along with a good splash of water. Bring to the boil, then cover and simmer for 5 minutes. The gravy should be creamy, not too thick or thin.

Vegetables

Serves 4–8

4 large or 8 small red or green peppers,
    tops cut off and seeds scooped out
3 tbsp vegetable oil
1 tsp cumin seeds
1 onion, peeled and chopped
3 large tomatoes, chopped
2 tsp finely chopped fresh ginger
2 good handfuls of frozen peas
70g green beans, chopped into small
    pieces

salt, to taste
$\frac{1}{4}$ tsp turmeric
$\frac{1}{4}$–$\frac{1}{2}$ tsp red chilli powder
2 tsp ground coriander
1$\frac{1}{2}$ tsp garam masala
250g paneer, ideally freshly made (see
    page 13)
5 tbsp double cream
handful of fresh coriander, chopped

Paneer-stuffed Peppers

Paneer scrambled and cooked with peppers was a regular at our table as I grew up. It is a delicate, simply spiced dish with the tartness of the tomatoes contrasting beautifully with the sweet onions and paneer. In this recipe I decided to stuff the peppers with the paneer instead of cooking them together, also adding extra vegetables to lighten the dish, making a great vegetarian main course. I recommend you make fresh paneer as shop-bought paneer can be a little rubbery and will not crumble in the same way. If you have no other option, cut the paneer into small cubes instead of crumbling. Serve one half for a small meal or satisfying starter or two for a main course with some naan, rice or salad. If you wish, stir 200g cooked rice into the filling mixture when you add the paneer for a complete meal.

Preheat the oven to 190°C/375°F/gas mark 5. Place the peppers on a baking tray and bake for 20–25 minutes or until soft.

Meanwhile, heat the oil in a non-stick pan. Add the cumin seeds and fry until they darken, around 20 seconds. Add the onion and cook until soft and golden. Add the tomatoes, ginger, peas, beans, salt and spices and cook until the tomatoes have softened, around 8–10 minutes.

Crumble in the paneer and add 100ml water; stir well to mix. Add the cream, check the seasoning and add a little more than you would normally as the pepper will absorb some. Add the coriander and enough water to the pan to be able to spoon in a tablespoon of liquid with every serving. The paneer will continue absorbing liquid, so add a little more, if necessary.

Halve the peppers. Fill the open halves with the paneer mixture, adding some of the gravy. Place under a preheated grill to brown the top before serving.

Serves 4

1½ tbsp vegetable oil
1 tsp cumin seeds
½ tsp brown mustard seeds
½ tsp turmeric
¼ tsp red chilli powder
1 rounded tsp ground coriander
salt, to taste
1 medium cucumber, peeled and sliced
    into thin half moons
120g frozen peas
3 rounded tbsp natural yoghurt, stirred well
1 tbsp shredded fresh mint leaves or
    1 tbsp good-quality dried mint

Lightly Spiced Cucumber, Peas and Mint

I didn't deliberately set out to be summery with this dish, but it somehow turned out that way. Cucumber is served as a hot vegetable in certain regions across India, cooked in yoghurt in the north and in coconut milk in the south. When cooked, it mutates into a delicate vegetable, lending itself wonderfully to accompanying lightly spiced dishes. The peas add wonderful bursts of sweetness in the slightly tart gravy. I think this is a great dish for a summery meal, whether it is full-on Indian or accompanying a Western-style grill or roast.

Heat the oil in a small non-stick saucepan and add the cumin and mustard seeds. Once they start to pop, add the remaining spices and salt and follow immediately with the cucumber. Cook over a moderate heat until the vegetable becomes slightly soft and translucent, around 4–5 minutes. Add the peas and cook for 2–3 minutes, just to heat through. Stir in the yoghurt and mint, cook for 2 minutes and serve.

Kashmiri Turnips

Serves 4

3 tbsp vegetable oil
pinch of asafoetida
¾ tsp cumin seeds
3 cloves
thumbnail-sized piece of cinnamon stick
700g turnips, peeled and cut into wedges
1½ tsp ginger paste
¼ tsp turmeric
1½ tsp ground coriander
¼–½ tsp red chilli powder
¾ tsp garam masala
salt, to taste
¾ tsp sugar, or to taste
large handful of fresh coriander leaves
        and stalks, chopped

The turnip is an underrated vegetable – I don't remember the last time I saw anyone cook with it outside of a North Indian home. It is a vegetable I grew up with and one I have, at times, eaten once a week. It is not an obvious vegetable choice and that is such a shame. We used to eat turnips Punjabi-style with onions, ginger, garlic and tomatoes – the colourful flavours of Punjab. In Kashmir, they use simple spices to coax out the inherent flavour of this humble vegetable. When buying turnips, look for the freshest, youngest ones, as they become fibrous with age.

Heat the oil in a large non-stick saucepan. Add the asafoetida, cumin, cloves and cinnamon. Once the cumin starts to colour, add the turnips and cook until starting to brown on the edges or sides, around 4–5 minutes, stirring often.

Add the remaining spices, salt and sugar, give the pan a stir and add enough water to come nearly halfway up the turnips. Bring to the boil, then cover and cook over a low heat until the turnips are tender, around 6–8 minutes or until the point of a knife goes through them. Do not overcook as they will start to break down. Uncover and dry off any excess water, if there is any.

Taste and adjust the salt and sugar, stir in the fresh coriander and serve.

Stir-fried Peppers with Gram Flour

Serves 4

3 tbsp vegetable oil
1½ tsp mustard seeds
½ tsp turmeric
½ tsp red chilli powder
1 tbsp ground coriander
salt, to taste
3 green peppers, cored and cut into 1cm cubes
5 tbsp gram flour
1½ tsp lemon juice, or taste

This is my favourite way to eat peppers. I generally find peppers a good vegetable to use as a secondary flavouring but not as the main ingredient, whether in a ratatouille, roasted in a salad or as a container to stuff with rice and meats. But having discovered this flavour combination, I actually miss this dish if I don't make it regularly, and everyone seems to love it. Green peppers work best with these flavours as the red versions tend to be sweeter. The gram flour adds a savoury element and the lemon juice lifts the whole dish. A great accompaniment that works well with both traditional meals and international dishes.

Heat the oil in a large non-stick frying pan. Add the mustard seeds. Once they start to pop, add all the spices and salt, lower the heat, and cook for 15 seconds. Add the peppers and stir-fry for 3 minutes or until starting to soften at the sides.

Add the gram flour and stir-fry for another 3 minutes or until you can smell the gram flour, which means it is now cooked. If you are not sure, stir-fry for another minute – the only thing that will happen is that the peppers will not have as much bite. Stir in the lemon juice and serve.

Above: Kashmiri Turnips
Below: Stir-fried Peppers with Gram Flour

3 tbsp vegetable oil
good pinch of asafoetida
1 bay leaf
¼ tsp panch phoran (see page 249)
1–2 mild dried red chillies
1 small onion, peeled and sliced
½ tsp turmeric
2 scant tsp ground cumin
1 rounded tsp ground coriander
salt, to taste
¾ tsp sugar, or to taste
2 tsp ginger paste
500g butternut squash, peeled, seeds removed and flesh cut into 4cm chunks
150–200g canned chickpeas, drained and rinsed
¾ tsp garam masala
¾ tsp fennel seeds, powdered

Bengali Squash with Chickpeas

Butternut squash is one of my favourite varieties of pumpkin as it is smoother and creamier than the large orange pumpkins we see at Halloween. It is a wonderful match for the earthiness of the chickpeas, especially when paired with these sweet and earthy spices. These ingredients and flavours have a definitive West Bengali flair. This is a fantastic vegetarian autumnal main course (add more beans or some cubes of paneer) or a great side dish to meat or chicken dishes. You can vary the beans (cannellini or butterbeans would also be delicious) or make it with sweet potatoes.

Heat the oil in a large non-stick saucepan. Add the asafoetida, bay leaf, panch phoran and chillies; cook over a low heat for about 1 minute.

Add the onion and cook until soft and golden. Stir in the turmeric, cumin and coriander, along with the salt, sugar and ginger paste. Give the pan a stir, add a splash of water and cook for another minute.

Add the squash, pour in 150ml water. Bring to the boil, then cover and simmer until the squash is cooked through, around 15–18 minutes.

Stir in the chickpeas, garam masala, fennel seed powder and a splash of water. Cook for another minute and serve. The dish should be moist but not gravied.

Serves 4

1½ tbsp vegetable or coconut oil
20 whole black peppercorns
1 large piece of cinnamon stick
2 cloves
1 small onion, peeled and sliced
15 curry leaves
3–5 green chillies, whole and pricked with
    the tip of a knife
12g fresh ginger, peeled and finely
    chopped

100g broccoli florets
100g cauliflower florets
100g frozen green beans
100g potato, peeled, boiled and mashed
100g frozen peas
250ml coconut milk
1 tsp garam masala
salt, to taste
250g rice noodles
handful of coriander leaves and stalks,
    chopped

Vegetables and Rice Noodles in a Coconut Broth

A subtle soupy dish which is actually a combination of two Keralan dishes – vegetable stew (ishtoo) and rice noodles (iddiapam). The vegetable stew is often eaten with a rice-based fluffy pancake, but the noodles make a lovely textural contrast and are just a lot easier. A great one-dish meal for people who love the flavours of the South. You can use any vegetables you like and can also add some leftover roasted or grilled chicken on the top.

Heat the oil in a large non-stick saucepan. Add the whole spices and fry for 20 seconds. Add the onion and fry until soft and lightly golden. Add the curry leaves, chillies and ginger and cook for 30 seconds. Season, add the broccoli and cauliflower and cover with water. Bring to the boil and cook until just tender, around 5–6 minutes.

Stir in the green beans, mashed potato and peas so that the potato thickens the water. Add the coconut milk and garam masala and loosen with enough water so the broth has the consistency of single cream. Bring to a gentle simmer, taste and adjust the seasoning.

Cook the noodles according to the packet instructions. Once cooked, drain and place directly into your serving bowls. Ladle over the stew. Sprinkle the coriander over the top and serve hot.

Serves 6

5 tbsp vegetable oil
⅛ tsp asafoetida
1 tsp mustard seeds
1 medium–large potato, peeled and cut
    into 4cm chunks
4 small aubergines, slit through the middle
1 medium–large parsnip, peeled and
    cut crosswise into 2.5cm discs and
    half-moons at the very top
1 medium sweet potato, peeled and cut
    into 4cm chunks
2 handfuls of frozen tuvar beans (from
    Indian shops) or frozen broad beans
    or peas

Masala

20g fresh ginger, peeled
2 large cloves of garlic, peeled
1–2 green chillies, deseeded
4 tsp lemon juice
40g fresh coriander leaves and stalks,
    chopped
2 rounded tsp ground coriander
1¼ tsp ground cumin
¾ tsp carom seeds
1½–2 tsp salt, or to taste
1 tbsp sugar
1 tbsp roasted peanuts, powdered (to help
    bind the gravy)
70g finely grated fresh or frozen coconut,
    plus extra to garnish

Gujarati Undhiyo

This is a traditional Gujarati dish and one I promise myself to make more regularly every time I eat it. It is full of flavour and a comforting autumnal dish. In the old days in Gujarat, it was made in a huge pot with the vegetables slashed at regular intervals, with the masala stuffed inside these tight crevasses to flavour them from the inside, and layered in accordance to their cooking time. It was cooked really slowly so that all the veg were cooked to succulent perfection. I almost left the traditional recipe unchanged for us non-Gujarati cooks, but I couldn't help myself. It is such a wonderful dish that I wanted to simplify it as much as possible to entice everyone to try it. It is fantastic just as it is, as part of an Indian meal or as an accompaniment to a roast dish. Fresh or frozen coconut is best, but you can use about 10 tablespoons of desiccated coconut instead. Lastly, for the full monty, add the fenugreek dumplings from the Lamb and Dumpling Stew on page 136 with the rest of the vegetables.

Using a blender, make a paste of the ginger, garlic, green chillies and lemon juice with a splash of water. Add most of the fresh coriander (reserving a little for garnish) and pulse to shred finely but not completely puréed. Stir in the remaining ingredients for the masala. Taste and make sure it is slightly over-seasoned as the vegetables will absorb some of it.

Heat the oil in a large non-stick saucepan. Add the asafoetida and fry for 20 seconds. Follow with the mustard seeds and, once they start to pop, add all the masala. Give the pan a good stir, Add all the vegetables except the beans or peas and stir into the spice paste for a few minutes. Add 200ml water and bring to the boil. Cover and cook over a low heat, shaking the pan occasionally. Once the vegetables are just soft, around 20–25 minutes, add the beans or peas, cover and cook for another 2–3 minutes. Serve garnished with the remaining coriander and coconut.

Spicy Keralan Mash

Serves 4

450g potatoes or tapioca
1½ tbsp vegetable oil
½ tsp each mustard seeds and cumin seeds
¾ tsp fennel seeds or powder
1 small onion, peeled and chopped
2 green chillies, whole but pricked with the tip of a knife or slit
15 curry leaves
2 cloves of garlic, peeled and finely chopped
1 tsp garam masala
salt and freshly ground black pepper, to taste
180–280ml milk (tapioca needs more than the potato)
3 tbsp double cream
3 tbsp grated fresh or desiccated coconut
1–2 tsp lemon juice, or to taste

The Keralans love mash. One of their staples is tapioca, a root vegetable similar to potato but with a different texture and a hint of coconut flavour. Tapioca is mainly found in ethnic markets, so I often use potato instead. I have added a little cream for some richness and have reduced the oil for this reason, but you can leave it out and increase the oil if you prefer. Indians do not expect or fret over perfect, lump-free mash, as a few bits of whole potato add texture. Once you have mashed the potato or tapioca, stir it as little as possible as overworking it will turn the mash gluey.

Peel the tapioca, if using, and cut into large cubes. Boil in plenty of water until soft. Boil the potatoes, if using, in large chunks until soft, then peel. Mash while hot.

Heat the oil in a small non-stick pan. Add the mustard and cumin seeds. When they start to pop, add fennel seeds (if using), onion and green chillies. When the onion has just softened, add the curry leaves and garlic and cook for 40 seconds or until just starting to colour.

Stir in the garam masala, salt and pepper, fennel seed powder (if using), milk, cream and coconut and bring to a gentle boil. Gently stir in the mash. Taste and adjust the seasoning and add lemon juice to taste.

Wild Mushrooms in Black Masala

Serves 4

1 tbsp Bengal gram lentils
2½ tbsp vegetable oil
1 tsp mustard seeds
450g wild mushrooms, cleaned with kitchen paper
salt, to taste
1½ tsp black masala, or to taste (see page 12)
½–¾ tsp tamarind paste, or to taste
small handful of fresh coriander leaves and stalks, chopped

I love the flavours of wild mushrooms – they might be more expensive than simpler closed-cup mushrooms but they do have a much deeper flavour. You don't need to use the really expensive mushrooms here; oyster, shiitake and other such mid-range fungi would give a great flavour and textural contrasts. The black masala is a store-cupboard basic for those from Maharashtra and is a blend of mild spices and dried coconut that have been roasted (see page 12). The resulting flavour is a wonderful, deep, sweet nuttiness. I add tamarind paste for a light tartness to bring out the earthy flavours, but for special occasions you can also add a spoon of crème fraîche for a richer dish. Serve as part of a meal, a side dish or for a decadent mushrooms-on-toast meal.

Dry-fry the lentils in a frying pan until they darken a little but before they become brown; grind to a powder.

Heat the vegetable oil in a large frying pan or karahi. Add the mustard seeds and once they start to pop, add the mushrooms and salt and sauté until all water they release has dried off. Add the black masala and lentil powder and fry along with the mushrooms for another 3 minutes. Stir in 50ml water and the tamarind paste and coriander; give the pan a good stir and serve.

Above: Spicy Keralan Mash
Below: Wild Mushrooms in Black Masala

Serves 6, can be halved

6 tbsp gram flour
3 tsp rice flour
salt, to taste
¼–½ tsp red chilli powder, to taste
2 tsp ground cumin
2 tsp ground coriander
¾ tsp dried mango powder
2 medium aubergines, cut crossways into
    slices 5mm thick
vegetable oil, as needed
15 fresh curry leaves to garnish (optional)

Goan Spiced Aubergine

The Goans tend to cook their vegetables quite simply (I think they prefer to spend their time cooking fish and meat dishes), but their sense of taste ensures that even when simply cooked, their vegetable dishes are still delicious, as are these spiced aubergines. If you wish, for added crunch, you can coat the battered aubergine slices lightly with semolina before cooking.

Preheat the oven to 160°C/325°F/gas mark 3.

Whisk together all the dry ingredients and slowly add 170–180ml water while whisking to make a thin batter. Taste and adjust the seasoning and spices, over-seasoning a little as the aubergine will draw the flavours out.

Heat enough oil for a 2.5mm film in a large non-stick frying pan. Dip the aubergine slices into the batter one by one and place in the pan (do not overcrowd). Cook over a low heat until golden brown on one side, around 2–3 minutes. Turn the aubergines over and cook the other side until soft all the way through. Drain on kitchen paper and place the plate in the oven to keep them warm while you cook the remaining aubergine slices.

Heat 1 teaspoon of oil in the frying pan and add the curry leaves. When they splutter, drain, toss in a little salt and scatter over the aubergines.

Goa

Goa conjures up images of white beaches peppered with small huts selling local snacks,

palms trees swaying in the breeze against the colourful Iberian-influenced architecture and fantastic, unique food. Goa has seen many settlers in her history but none has laid their mark as the Portuguese have. They remained there for hundreds of years and changed Goan food, and indeed Indian food, forever.

The Portuguese settlers introduced foods they had discovered on their travel – chillies, tomatoes, sweet potatoes, cashews, pineapples and even certain varieties of mangoes. They also brought with them their own new meats (pork and beef), wine, breads and pastries. They taught the locals how to cook their food properly and these cooks soon became prized finds and were sought after by the wealthy non-Indians across the country so they could eat food that was not a 'curry' and impress their guests with delicious dishes and fresh breads.

One of the main reasons this food became part of the fabric of the local cuisine was the large number of people who converted to Catholicism in the region. They were no longer forbidden by religion to eat these meats. In fact, they soon gained a taste for them and before too long the cuisine was changed forever. Those who remained Hindu resisted the Portuguese influence and their food remains largely authentic to the area with

the convenient exceptions of happily substituting the pepper they traditionally used (called long pepper) for the new chillies (they prefer to use red chillies and these vary from the large, mild and red ones to the small and fiery ones). The locals also adopted tomatoes, which were used with the tamarind to sour their dishes.

Their food still has a very different feel to that of their Portuguese brothers, although both live in harmony with each other and share the same love of the local fish, spices and the quintessential Goan ingredient – the coconut.

The Goans love their food just as much as they love their siestas; they are a laid-back people, as befits those who live by the sea, and they are always nostalgic for food from their childhood. Whilst we cannot recreate the authentic experience of eating a meal in Goa, we can definitely get a flavour of their food and thus the people.

Try the Goan Fish Curry (page 59), Baked Chutney-stuffed Fish (page 67) or the Coconut and Chilli Okra (page 164) to sample the local dishes eaten in Hindu homes. And for the Portuguese Goan dishes, try making the Prawn Toasts (page 32), Red Goan Chicken (page 94), Pork Vindaloo (page 125), and one of my favourite desserts, Coconut Bebinca (page 241).

Serves 4–6

3 tbsp vegetable oil
1½ tsp coriander seeds
1¼ tsp mustard seeds
1 tsp urad dal lentils
2–4 dried red chillies
½ tsp cumin seeds
3 cloves of garlic, peeled and sliced
1 tsp chopped fresh ginger
400g okra, topped and cut into 2.5cm
    pieces
90g fresh or frozen finely grated coconut
salt, to taste
100ml coconut milk
1¼ tsp tamarind paste

Coconut and Chilli Okra

This is a typical dish made at home in the south. It is quick and easy and tastes delicious. It might not be the kind of dish you find in a restaurant but that is a shame, as simple flavours without excess frying have a place in Indian restaurants. Okra is really good for you and has lots of calcium, so I like to make it every now and again. I decided to make it with some strong flavours but few spices and it is just delicious. Give it a try.

Heat 1 teaspoon of the oil in a small pan and add the coriander and mustard seeds, lentils and the red chillies. Once the mustard seeds start to pop, take off the heat and grind to a powder.

Heat the remaining oil in a wide sauté pan. Add the cumin seeds and once they have browned a little, add the garlic and ginger; stir-fry for 30 seconds. Add the okra and stir fry until soft, around 7–8 minutes. Add the powdered spices, grated coconut and salt and stir-fry for another 3–4 minutes. Add the coconut milk and tamarind paste and cook for 1–2 minutes, then serve.

Green Beans with Lentils

Serves 4

250g green beans, topped and tailed and sliced
    crossways into 1cm pieces
pinch of sugar
50g yellow split mung lentils, rinsed well and soaked
    for 30 minutes
2 tbsp coconut oil or vegetable oil
1 tsp mustard seeds
1 rounded tsp split black gram
15 curry leaves
1 green chilli, chopped (optional)
2 dried red chillies, whole
salt, to taste
1 tbsp fresh or frozen grated coconut (optional)

This is a dish that doesn't punch any flavours but the combination and textures ensure that you come back for another spoonful. The coconut oil adds a wonderful coastal flavour to this simple dish, but if you don't have any, try to add a little fresh or frozen coconut in at the end to introduce that coconut flavour. The dish can be made without either, but will benefit from at least one or the other. If you do cook with coconut oil, you need to know that the overtly sun-tanning lotion smell that is so pronounced goes away completely when cooked and is replaced with a subtle reminder of the provenance of the dish.

Cook the green beans in salted water with a pinch of sugar for 3–5 minutes, then drain. Boil the drained lentils in fresh water until just soft, around 12 minutes. Drain again.

Heat the oil in a small non-stick saucepan. Add the mustard seeds and cook over a low heat, until they splutter. Add the black gram and fry until just changing colour, 30 seconds or so. Throw in the curry leaves and follow 5 seconds later with the fresh and dried chillies; stir-fry for 20 seconds. Add the beans, lentils and salt and stir fry to heat though and for the flavours to mix well. Serve garnished with the coconut.

Stir-fried Peas

Serves 4

3–4 tbsp vegetable oil
1 tsp brown mustard seeds
1 tsp cumin seeds
15 curry leaves
1½ tsp ginger paste
1 green chilli, deseeded and made into a paste,
    or 2 whole green chillies pricked with the tip
    of a knife
salt, to taste
250g fresh or frozen green peas, thawed and
    roughly chopped
6 tbsp milk
¾–1 tsp lemon juice, or to taste (optional)

This dish is often served as a snack topped with crisp, fried, shredded potatoes, but as we seldom have a mid-afternoon savoury snack with our tea, it has been adapted to be eaten with a meal. It also makes a lovely samosa filling or a great side dish with fish. I sometimes chop the peas before cooking them, partly because that was how this dish was first introduced to me and partly because the savoury flavours manage to get right inside the vegetables, rather than just a thin outer coating. You can cook them whole, then gently mash them in the pan; it won't have the same texture but the flavours will be right. Add lemon juice to taste; sometimes I leave it out, but at other times I like to balance the sweetness with the tartness.

Heat the oil in a small non-stick saucepan. Add the seeds and once they splutter and pop, around 20 seconds, throw in the curry leaves. Follow 10 seconds later with the ginger and chilli pastes; stir-fry for 20 seconds.

Add the salt and peas and stir-fry for 10 seconds. Pour in the milk and cook, covered, for 5–6 minutes or until the peas are tender and the milk has been absorbed. Stir in the lemon juice, if using, and serve.

Above: Stir-fried Peas
Below: Green Beans with Lentils

vegetable oil, for deep-frying
450g potatoes, peeled and cut into
    finger-sized chips
1$\frac{1}{4}$ tsp cumin seeds
30g cashew nuts
1 rounded tbsp sesame seeds
$\frac{1}{2}$ tsp turmeric
$\frac{1}{4}$–$\frac{1}{2}$ tsp red chilli powder, or to taste
salt, to taste
1 tsp sugar, or to taste
$\frac{3}{4}$ tsp dried mango powder

Gujarati Chips with Cashew Nuts

I know this sounds like it is entirely my recipe for chips, but that would be taking credit where it is not due. This is my version of an existing Gujarati dish in which potatoes are fried and given a 'tarka' of the flavours. The potatoes are crispy, which is further accentuated with the bite of the cumin and sesame seeds and the odd cashew nut. The sugar may seem odd in chips but somehow it just works. These are salty, spicy, slightly sweet and entirely moreish. Do use a large pan or cook the potatoes in two batches as overcrowding the pan often leads to chips that do not stay crisp. Cooking the chips twice also helps them to stay crisp longer.

Heat the oil in a large, deep saucepan. Add the potatoes and fry over a low–moderate heat until just cooked, around 5 minutes. Check with the point of a knife. Remove with a slotted spoon and place in a sieve. Once the chips have cooled, reheat the oil and cook the chips for a second time until golden and crisp, another 2–3 minutes. Place in a sieve so any excess oil drips off.

Meanwhile, heat 1 teaspoon of oil in a small frying pan or saucepan. Add the cumin seeds and cook for 10 seconds or until aromatic. Add the cashew nuts and follow 30 seconds later with the sesame seeds. Once coloured, add the remaining spices and seasonings, stir well to mix and toss with the cooked potatoes in the sieve. Serve immediately.

Beans and Lentils

Jain Bengal Gram Curry

Serves 4–6

200g Bengal gram, washed and soaked
    overnight or for the day
2 tbsp vegetable oil
pinch of asafoetida
1 tsp cumin seeds
1 tsp turmeric
¾ tsp red chilli powder
2 tsp ground coriander
salt, to taste
3 tbsp natural yoghurt, whisked in a bowl with a couple
    of spoons of water
½ tsp garam masala

My in-laws are Jain – a beautiful religion founded on non-violence and sharing similar values to Hinduism. Most Jains are strictly vegetarian, shunning not only all red and white meats, fish and eggs, but also onions and garlic as they are said to hinder spiritual thoughts. Once you start exploring this, you realise that simplicity should not be confused with unrefined. The mark of a great cook is said to be one who has the confidence to cook with fewer rather than more ingredients. I feel that many dishes from this cuisine show generations of true masters. This dish is delicious, simple, easy and quick to cook. You will need the foresight to soak the lentils well in advance.

Heat the oil in a large frying pan. Add the asafoetida and allow to fry for a few seconds. Add the cumin seeds and once they start to darken, add the drained lentils and enough water to just cover them. Add the turmeric, chilli powder and ground coriander. Bring to the boil and simmer over a moderately high heat until the lentils are cooked and al dente – no crunch but soft and whole. This can take from 5 to 10 minutes, depending how fresh they are and how long they have been soaked for.

Stir in the salt, yoghurt and garam masala, cover and cook for another 2–4 minutes, stirring often. Serve with Indian bread.

Bengali Red Lentils

Serves 4–5

250g red lentils, rinsed until the water runs clear
salt, to taste
½ tsp turmeric
¼ – ½ tsp red chilli powder
1 tbsp ghee
2 dried red chillies
1 rounded tsp panch phoran (see page 249)

These lentils are everyday fare in Bengal and this recipe shows how sometimes all you really need are a few ingredients to produce a stellar dish. The flavours are of the ghee, panch phoran and lentils and that is enough. It is a light dish as this lentil is easy on the system, offers a good source of protein for vegetarians and is one of the quickest cooking lentils in India. You can eat this dish with rice or flat-breads as a meal or as an accompaniment.

Bring 1 litre of water to the boil in a large saucepan. Stir in the lentils, salt, turmeric and chilli powder. Bring back to the boil, then simmer over a moderate heat until the lentils are soft, around 20 minutes. Some will start to break up while others remain whole and the lentils will become indistinct from the water.

Heat the ghee in a small saucepan. Add the red chillies and panch phoran. Fry for 20 seconds and pour in to the lentils. Stir well, taste and adjust the seasoning, then loosen with a little water from a recently boiled kettle, if necessary – it should be a thickish curry.

Above: Bengali Red Lentils
Below: Jain Bengal Gram Curry

125g yellow split mung lentils, washed
     and soaked for 1 hour
7g fresh ginger, peeled and chopped
1–2 green chillies, deseeded and chopped
¼ tsp turmeric
salt, to taste
1 large tomato, roughly chopped
2 tbsp oil
1 tsp cumin seeds
6 curry leaves, shredded
3 large cloves of garlic, peeled and
     roughly sliced
handful of fresh coriander, chopped

Easy Mung Lentil Curry

This is a simple but utterly delicious lentil curry that is often served in the homes of
Sindhis, a group of people who hail from the northern region of Sindh, which is now part
of Pakistan. However, this wholesome, homely dish could almost hail from any community.
It is easy to make and appeals to all. It is a loose curry, so serve it with some plain basmati
rice on the side.

Place the drained lentils, ginger, chillies, turmeric, salt, tomato and 750ml water in a large saucepan. Bring to the
boil, then turn the heat down and simmer for 30–40 minutes or until the lentils have softened and the water has
turned yellow and slightly creamy from some of the lentils breaking down. The curry will thicken further as it cools,
so if you are serving the reheated curry later, add an extra splash of boiled water to the pot.

Heat the oil in a small saucepan. Add the cumin seeds and once they release their aroma, stir in the curry leaves
and garlic. When the garlic starts to brown at the edges, pour it all into the lentils along with the chopped coriander.
Stir well and serve.

250g Bengal gram, rinsed until the water
   runs clear
3 tbsp vegetable oil
1 tbsp cumin seeds
1 small onion, peeled and chopped
3–4 green chillies, left whole or slit (for heat)
20g fresh ginger, peeled and cut into
   julienne strips
2 fat cloves of garlic, peeled
3 large tomatoes
salt, to taste
$\frac{3}{4}$ tsp turmeric
$\frac{3}{4}$ tsp garam masala
$1\frac{1}{2}$ tsp ground coriander
handful of fresh coriander leaves and
   stalks, chopped

Tarka Dal

'Tarka' simply means a spiced, flavoured butter or oil that is cooked separately from the lentils and poured in at the end. The tarka changes depending on your mood, which region of India the lentil is from, and which lentil you are cooking. You can choose any kind of lentil and every home has its own preferred combination of spices and flavourings. In the UK a lot of these recipes seem to use red lentils, but I prefer the robust Bengal gram which stand up better to these north Indian flavours. I sometimes stir in a spoon of ghee just before serving as it has a wonderful aroma and buttery flavour that makes the dish that bit more special.

Place the lentils and 1 litre of water in a deep saucepan. Bring to the boil, then skim off the froth that appears on the surface. Cover and simmer over a moderate heat until the Bengal gram is just soft, around 40 minutes. Add more water if the pan gets dry. Use a whisk to break up some of the lentils so that the water becomes yellow and thick. It will thicken as it sits.

Meanwhile, heat the oil in a small non-stick saucepan. Add the cumin seeds and cook until they release their distinctive aroma, around 30 seconds. Add the onion, green chillies and ginger and cook until golden, around 8–10 minutes.

Using a blender, purée the garlic and tomatoes together. Add to the onions with the salt, powdered spices and 100ml water. Cook over a moderate heat for 15–20 minutes until the masala releases its oil.

Stir into the cooked lentils. Add more water if the curry is too thick. Bring to the boil, taste and adjust the seasoning. Stir in the fresh coriander and serve.

250g whole masoor (brown) lentils, rinsed
6g fresh ginger, peeled
4 fat cloves of garlic, peeled
3 tbsp vegetable oil
2 tsp cumin seeds
½ small onion, peeled and chopped
salt, to taste
1 rounded tsp ground coriander
½ tsp garam masala
½ tsp red chilli powder, or to taste
½ tsp turmeric
3 small tomatoes, puréed
handful of fresh coriander leaves and
    stalks, chopped

Whole Brown Lentil Curry

This lentil curry is absolutely delicious; it is so thick and wholesome and flavourful that I do not know anyone who does not like it. When this lentil is split and the skin removed, it produces the little red lentils we are used to seeing and eating. They are light and easy to digest. The only drawback is that they take a while to cook, but they are certainly worth the wait. Make sure there is enough water in the pan.

Place the lentils and 1.1 litres of water in a large saucepan, bring to the boil, then simmer, covered, until they are soft, around 50–60 minutes. Give an occasional stir to make sure the lentils do not settle at the bottom of the pan.

Meanwhile, using a blender, make a paste of the ginger and garlic with a splash of water.

Heat the oil in a small non-stick saucepan. Add the cumin seeds and cook until you can smell their aroma. Add the onion and cook until golden brown. Pour in the ginger and garlic paste and cook until the paste has become golden and you can smell the cooked garlic. Add the salt and the powdered spices and stir for 10 seconds.

Pour in the tomatoes and simmer over a moderate heat, covered, until all the excess moisture has boiled off. Fry for another 3–4 minutes or until the oil comes out from the masala. Taste – the masala should be smooth to taste; if not, cook for another few minutes, stirring often. Stir into the cooked lentils and simmer for another 10 minutes. Taste, adjust the seasoning, then stir in the fresh coriander and serve.

Gujarat

Many of us may never have eaten a proper Gujarati meal,

although we might have nibbled on the wonderful, quintessentially Gujarati snacks such as *dhokla* (a light, steamed, spongy lentil cake), *muthiya* (a gram flour and vegetable dumpling) and, of course, the much-loved onion bhaji. For a real understanding of the flavours, though, you will need to be invited into their homes, and as the people from this western state are warm, hospitable and generous, they are generally happy to receive guests.

Their food will vary depending on where in Gujarat they are from and if they are Hindu or Muslim. Hindus are mainly vegetarian and Muslim non-vegetarian. The different areas of Gujarat have varying geographies and climates; some are dry so have few fresh vegetables but lots of dairy, while others are spoiled for choice with a variety of different grains and vegetables. Some add jaggery to their food, others don't. Some, who live by the sea will have a diet rich in fish, even if they are Hindus. This is regional food within a region.

Many vegetarians are so strict that they will even shun onions and garlic as these are said to slow down spiritual progress. Meals are based on vegetables, lentils, rice and breads. It is to their credit that with all these restrictions, they manage to produce food that is so delicious. Fresh coconut and coriander are often added for flavour and texture, and asafoetida for its pungent flavour as well as its digestive properties. The

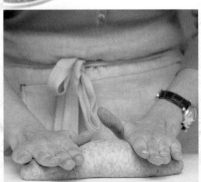

resulting flavours are a subtle balance of salt, spice, sour and sweet. The cuisine seems to have been shaped by busy mothers, as most dishes are easy to cook and there are many one-pot meals, each with a different combination of carbohydrates (rice or wheat), protein (lentils) and vegetables. It may sound unsophisticated but it is, in fact, very well balanced, well flavoured and delicate. When entertaining, a meal would have been served on steel plates, *thalis*, and would consist of a bread, vegetables, lentils, chutneys or pickles, something sweet and a savoury snack. It will all be washed down with cumin-spiced buttermilk and taste absolutely delicious.

The non-vegetarian dishes are just as fantastic. There are light chicken curries, complex biryanis and moist kebabs, and while these will have stronger flavours than the vegetarian dishes, they are still lighter than many other Muslim dishes across India. Over the centuries Gujaratis have emigrated all over the world, some to Pakistan or east Africa, others to England, but wherever they go and in whichever climate they find themselves, their food stills bear the footprints of Gujarat.

For the flavours of this region, try Steamed Spinach and Rice Dumplings (see page 22), Spongy Lentil Cake (see page 42), Lamb and Dumpling Stew (see page 136), Undhiyo (see page 157), Sweet and Sour Lentils with Peanuts (see page 188) and Bhakri (see page 208).

Serves 4–6

4 tbsp vegetable oil
2 bay leaves
2 tsp cumin seeds
2 green chillies, left whole or slit
1 small–medium onion, peeled and
    chopped
17g fresh ginger, peeled
5 cloves of garlic, peeled
½ tsp turmeric
¼–½ tsp red chilli powder
1 tbsp ground coriander
1 tsp garam masala
salt, to taste
3 large tomatoes, puréed
2 x 410g tins of black-eyed peas, drained
    and rinsed
handful of fresh coriander leaves and
    stalks, chopped

Black-eyed Pea Curry

This is a typical North Indian bean curry and tastes so much better than it sounds. These versatile beans are full of good protein and are much meatier in flavour than the more humble lentils. Like kidney beans, black-eyed peas are often sold dried, needing to be soaked overnight and boiled before using, but the canned ones work well too and I often find myself turning to them in times of spontaneity. This is one of my favourite bean curries and it works equally well with rice as it does with Indian bread. It's also great part-puréed into a hearty soup with a swirl of yoghurt and some fresh wholegrain bread on the side.

Heat the oil in a medium-sized non-stick saucepan. Add the bay leaves and fry for 20 seconds, then add the cumin seeds and fry until they sizzle. Add the green chillies and onion and cook until well browned.

Meanwhile, using a blender, make a paste of the ginger and garlic with a splash of water. Stir into the pan and cook for about 1–2 minutes or until you can smell the cooked garlic. Add the powdered spices and salt and stir for another 30 seconds or so before pouring in the tomatoes. Cook over a medium heat until the oil leaves the masala, around 12–15 minutes.

Add the drained beans and mix well in the masala. Cook for a couple of minutes before pouring in 250ml water. Bring to the boil and simmer for 8–10 minutes. Take 2 tablespoons of the beans out of the gravy, mash well and stir back in. Stir in the fresh coriander and serve.

Serves 2–3

1½ tbsp vegetable oil
¾ tsp mustard seeds
6 curry leaves
½ tsp split black gram
3 tbsp finely chopped onion
1 green chilli, left whole or chopped if
    you like the bite
1 tsp finely chopped fresh ginger
1 tbsp chopped green mango (optional)
salt, to taste
½ small tomato, chopped
400g tin of butterbeans, drained and
    rinsed
1 tsp lemon or lime juice or to taste
2 tbsp fresh or frozen grated coconut
    or 1 tbsp desiccated coconut

Butterbean Sundal

This is a quick, easy and satisfying snack that is generally eaten on certain festivals in the south but delicious enough to feature at any time. A sundal is generally a quick, spicy snack made with any bean or lentil. It is often made without onions, as Hindus do not eat onions or garlic on holy days; instead, they add a pinch of asafoetida which has a strong pungency. This is my quick and easy version made with onions, which you can leave out if you wish. I sometimes add some fresh, soft salad leaves to the beans and serve it as a warm, healthy, protein-packed salad.

Heat the oil in a small non-stick saucepan, add the mustard seeds and fry until they pop. Stir in the curry leaves and lentils, then cook until the lentils colour a little, around 20 seconds. Add the onion and chilli and cook until soft and translucent.

Add the ginger, green mango, salt and tomato; cook, stirring frequently for 2–3 minutes. Add the butter beans, lemon juice and coconut and cook to heat through. Serve hot or warm as a snack. Alternatively, leave to cool a little and stir in some salad leaves.

Serves 4–6

4 tbsp vegetable oil
good pinch of asafoetida
1 tsp mustard seeds
14 curry leaves
1 small–medium onion, peeled and
    chopped
3g fresh ginger, peeled and finely chopped
5 large cloves of garlic, peeled and chopped
salt, to taste
½ tsp turmeric
½ tsp red chilli powder

1 rounded tsp ground coriander
150ml coconut milk
2 x 400g cans cannellini beans, drained
    and rinsed
10 cherry tomatoes, halved if large or left
    whole if small
1 tsp jaggery or sugar
¼–½ tsp tamarind paste, to taste (some
    brands are really strong)
handful of fresh or frozen grated coconut,
    to garnish
handful of fresh coriander, chopped

Cannellini Bean Curry

This bean curry is smooth, creamy, slightly sweet and lightly coconutty. It makes a great accompaniment to any southern Indian meal or is delicious as a vegetarian meal with some vegetables on the side. I sometimes eat leftovers with a hunk of bread or purée them into a thick, smooth soup and eat it in autumn. You can also dry off the water and make it into a wonderful mash – its virtues are endless. This dish hails from the south, where they use a sweet local white bean that is harder to find, but tinned cannellini beans make a wonderful substitute.

Heat the oil in a large non-stick saucepan. Add the asafoetida and, once it sizzles, add the mustard seeds. Once they start to pop, add the curry leaves, then the onion and cook until these are soft and golden, around 8–10 minutes. Add the ginger and garlic and cook for 1 minute over a moderate heat. Add the salt and powdered spices and stir for 30 seconds. Add the coconut milk and 200ml water and bring to the boil, then simmer for 10 minutes.

Add the beans and tomatoes and simmer for 5 minutes, allowing the flavours to marry. Stir in the sugar and tamarind paste, then mash some beans against the side of the pan to thicken the curry a little. Taste and adjust the tartness, sweetness and seasoning to taste. Garnish with the grated coconut and fresh coriander and serve.

Serves 4–6

200g split pigeon peas (tuvar dal),
    rinsed well
7g fresh ginger, peeled
1 large tomato, quartered
2 tbsp raw or roasted peanuts
1½–1¾ tbsp sugar or jaggery, to taste
½ tsp turmeric
¼–½ tsp red chilli powder or 2–3 round
    red chillies or dried red chillies
1 rounded tsp garam masala
salt, to taste
5–6 tsp lemon juice, or to taste

Tarka
2 tbsp ghee or vegetable oil
pinch of asafoetida
½ tsp mustard seeds
½ tsp cumin seeds
2 cloves
1 small piece of cinnamon stick
8 curry leaves

Sweet and Sour Lentils with Peanuts

This is a typical Gujarati lentil dish. It is slightly sweetened with jaggery and soured with either lemon juice or a sour fruit called cocum, which I love but is quite hard to find. If you do find either fresh or dried cocum, add five fruits with the tomatoes and let it cook with the lentils. In this case, add lemon juice to taste. The peanuts add a wonderful textural contrast and are often added raw, but sometimes it is easier to buy roasted, so add those instead but at the end so they do not alter the flavour of the dish too much. Always make sure there is enough water in the lentils, and add extra towards the end if the curry is looking too thick – this dish has a thinner consistency than those we see in most Indian restaurants here. Add as much sugar and lemon juice as you like – follow my guidelines, then taste and decide.

Place the lentils and 900ml water in a large saucepan. Bring to the boil, then skim off any froth and simmer until soft, around 20–30 minutes. Blend to a smooth paste with a hand blender.

Meanwhile, blend the ginger and tomato to a smooth paste. Add to the cooked lentils with the peanuts, sugar, turmeric, chilli powder (or chillies), garam masala, salt and lemon juice.

Heat the ghee or oil in a small saucepan. Add the asafoetida and cook for 5 seconds. Add the whole spices and allow to cook for 40 seconds over a low heat or until the mustard seeds pop. Add the curry leaves, let them crackle, then pour into lentils. Simmer for another 10 minutes. Add extra hot water from a recently boiled kettle to loosen, if necessary, then serve.

Rice and Bread

Serves 6–8

350g basmati rice
1 tbsp black peppercorns
4 black cardamom pods
4 bay leaves
6 large cloves of garlic, peeled and halved
4 x 5cm pieces of cinnamon stick
6 green cardamom pods

4 cloves
650g pieces of bone-in lamb (see page 10)
2 small–medium onions, peeled and sliced
12g fresh ginger, peeled and quartered
1½ tsp salt
4 tbsp vegetable oil
2 tsp cumin seeds
2–4 green chillies, slit

Lamb Pilaff

This is an absolutely delicious pilaff, known as a Lucknowi Biryani. The lamb is cooked in a spiced and flavoured broth to create a wonderful, deep and flavourful, but not spicy lamb stock. It is the meaty version of chicken soup for the soul – comforting and warming. The basmati rice is then cooked in this meaty broth to create a dish full of flavour. It is a classic recipe which is subtle to taste and easy to cook. You do, however, need the whole spices and good-quality lamb pieces with their bone in, as it is the bone that flavours the stock and therefore the rice. I usually use leg of lamb, but you can use shoulder. The best place to buy this lamb is from the butcher who will prepare the meat for you, as supermarkets seldom stock it on their shelves. Believe me, it is worth the trip.

Wash the rice in several changes of fresh water until the water runs clear. Leave to soak for 30 minutes.

Place all the spices, except the cumin seeds, on a small square of muslin, gather into a pouch and tie a knot. Place in a large saucepan with the lamb, one of the onions, the garlic, ginger, salt and 500ml water. Bring to the boil, then turn the heat down, cover, and simmer for 35–40 minutes or until the lamb is tender.

Once the lamb is done, remove the pieces of meat from the pan and strain the stock from the solids, pressing down on the solids to extract as much flavour as possible. Discard the solids and pour the stock into a measuring jug. Top up with enough water to measure 700ml.

Heat the oil in a large lidded pot. Add the cumin seeds and, once they sizzle, add the chillies and the remaining onion and cook until soft, around 6–7 minutes. Add the lamb pieces and brown for 2–3 minutes. Stir in the drained rice and add the reserved liquid.

Taste the stock and adjust the salt and chilli to taste. Bring the pan up to the boil, then reduce the heat to very low, cover with foil and a tightly fitting lid and cook for 8–10 minutes. Turn the heat off and leave to steam for another 5–10 minutes, then serve.

Serves 6

3 tbsp vegetable oil
750g jointed pieces of chicken, skinned
salt, to taste
1–2 tbsp lemon juice
butter, for greasing
3 sprigs of fresh coriander, 3 fresh mint
  leaves, 3 fresh basil leaves, 2 sprigs
  of fresh tarragon, all chopped together

Masala

120g fresh coriander leaves and stems
3 sprigs of fresh mint, leaves only
15 large basil leaves
3 sprigs of fresh tarragon
1 large onion, peeled, cut into large chunks
5 large cloves of garlic, peeled
7g fresh ginger, peeled or scrubbed
2–4 green chillies, or to taste
1 heaped tbsp ground coriander
1 tbsp white poppy seeds
1 black cardamom pod
8 small cloves
1 small shaving of cassia bark or cinnamon
  stick

Pilaff

1 generous tbsp ghee or vegetable oil
1 small piece of cinnamon stick
4 cloves
1 bay leaf
5 black peppercorns
1 black cardamom
1 small onion, peeled and sliced
300g basmati rice, rinsed well and soaked
  for 30 minutes
salt, to taste

Green Chicken Biryani

This unusual biryani is from one of the south-western regions of India and is a spectacular dish that deserves to be better known. A few years ago, a friend of mine kept talking about her mother's fantastic green chicken biryani. Out of curiosity, I gave it a try and have loved it ever since. It is a lot lighter and fresher than a traditional biryani but I find it equally satisfying and tasty. The list of ingredients may seem long but it is one of the quickest and easiest biryanis to make and is sure to impress. I have added some fresh soft herbs that are not Indian but really enhance the dish. I highly recommend you try this dish at least once.

Put all the masala ingredients into a food processor and blend into a fine paste.

Heat the 3 tablespoons of vegetable oil in a large non-stick saucepan. Add the chicken and sear on all sides over a high heat, about 2 minutes. Stir in the masala paste, 200ml water and salt. Bring to the boil, then cover and cook over a low heat until the chicken is cooked through, about 25–35 minutes, depending on the size of the chicken joints. Squeeze over the lemon juice to taste and make sure that the curry is well seasoned as it will seem less so when mixed with the rice. There should be plenty of gorgeous green gravy but it should not be watery; if it is, boil over a high heat for a couple of minutes to dry some off.

Meanwhile, heat the ghee or oil in another large non-stick saucepan. Add the whole spices and the onion and cook over a medium heat until well browned. Add the drained rice and cook for 1–2 minutes, stirring often, before adding 550ml water. Season with salt, tasting the water to make sure it is enough. Bring to a boil and then bring the heat down completely, cover and cook for 7–8 minutes. Try a grain, it should be just cooked but not soft. Take off the heat and leave to steam for 3 minutes with the lid on and another 3 minutes with it off.

Grease a large lidded baking dish with butter. Spoon in half the rice, top with the chicken, then the fresh herbs and finally the remaining rice. This can be kept for a few hours until cooking time or even covered and placed in the fridge overnight. When ready to cook, preheat the oven to 200°C/400°F/gas mark 6. Dot the butter evenly over the surface of the rice, cover well with foil and then the lid so the steam stays within. Place in the oven and heat through for 15 minutes if it is freshly prepared or up to 40 minutes if it is cold. Serve hot.

Serves 4

300g basmati rice, rinsed well and ideally
    soaked for 30 minutes
4 tbsp vegetable oil
1 medium–large onion, peeled, ½ cut
    into large chunks for the paste and
    ½ sliced
8g fresh ginger, peeled

4 large cloves of garlic, peeled
2 medium tomatoes, quartered
2 bay leaves
2.5cm piece of cinnamon stick
1 brown cardamom pod
6 green cardamom pods
5 cloves
salt, to taste
½ tsp turmeric

½–¾ tsp red chilli powder, or to taste
2 tsp ground coriander
1 tsp garam masala
2 rounded tbsp natural yoghurt
6 large eggs, boiled for 8 minutes, cooled,
    peeled and halved lengthways
15g butter, cut into small cubes
1 tbsp chopped fresh coriander leaves

Egg Biryani

I love egg curry and I think it works best with rice, so this recipe was hardly inspiration – it came about while thinking about what to make for lunch. I made a pilaff, which has since morphed into a biryani as it looks better and the eggs still resemble eggs in the final dish. This is, however, a simplified version of the great dish, as making a true biryani would mean more ingredients and more stages and I'm not convinced that this dish needs to be that elaborate. To make the dish more special, cook the rice in 1½ tablespoons of oil in which you have already fried a few green cardamoms, cloves, a single black cardamom and small piece of cinnamon (see below for method). You can garnish by drizzling over 1½ tablespoons of hot milk that has been infused with a pinch of saffron as well as scattering over roasted or fried almonds before the final cooking. Either way, it is a delicious, nutritious dish.

Drain the rice, then boil in a pan of water until it is nearly done (if you crush a grain in your fingers it will have a thin white line still in the middle), around 5–6 minutes of boiling if soaked and 8–9 minutes if not soaked. Drain and set aside.

Heat the oil in a large non-stick saucepan, stir in the sliced onion and cook until brown and becoming crisp at the edges. Drain the onions and keep aside. Meanwhile, using a blender, make a fine paste of the remaining onion, ginger, garlic and tomatoes.

Reheat the oil in the pan, add the bay leaves and whole spices and fry for 20 seconds or until they start to crackle. Pour in the paste along with a good splash of water, the salt and all the powdered spices. Stir well to mix and cook over a high heat until all the excess moisture has dried off, then reduce the heat and fry the paste until cooked through, around 10 minutes in total. Taste – it should have no harsh elements. Add the yoghurt and stir in to incorporate fully. Add 150ml water and bring to the boil. Taste and adjust the seasoning, over-seasoning a little to compensate for the rice and eggs.

Remove the curry mixture from the pan and give the pan a quick rinse. Add half the rice, layer with most of the curry and place the eggs on top, cut side up. Spoon over the remaining curry, scatter over the fried onions and finish with the remaining rice. Scatter the butter randomly over the surface. Cover tightly and place over a low heat for another 10 minutes or until the rice is fully cooked through. Scatter with the chopped coriander and serve.

Serves 4 as a meal

3 tbsp vegetable oil or ghee
1 tsp mustard seeds
¾ tsp cumin seeds
10 curry leaves
1 small onion, peeled and thinly sliced
2 cloves of garlic, peeled
7g fresh ginger, peeled
salt, to taste
¼ tsp red chilli powder
2–3 tsp black masala (see page 12)
    or 1 tsp garam masala
2 tbsp fresh or frozen grated coconut
    or 1 tbsp desiccated
200g rice, rinsed, drained and patted dry
good handful of frozen peas
1 carrot, peeled and coarsely grated
50g tiny cauliflower florets
2 tbsp cashew nuts, roasted or lightly fried
½–¾ tsp lemon juice, or to taste
handful of fresh coriander, chopped

Maharashtran One-Pot Rice

Even though I know this dish is often served on formal occasions, to me this dish is pure, homely comfort food where I would ring the changes depending on what I have in the fridge. This is a delicious rice dish that a mother would have waiting for her children with a warm hug. It is meant to be a vegetarian dish, but there is no reason why you couldn't add some leftover chicken or lamb for added protein or even some paneer or tofu. The black masala has become one of my favourite spice blends, which is saying something as I have grown up in a world where garam masala is king, but this sweet and spicy blend is so versatile and so flavourful that I am keen on adding it to everything on my table. If you have not made yours yet, you can still make the rice either with some garam masala or leave it out.

Heat the oil in a medium–large, lidded saucepan. Add the mustard and cumin seeds and, when they pop, stir in the curry leaves. Follow immediately with the onion and cook until golden.

Meanwhile, using a blender, make a paste of the garlic and ginger with a splash of water. Add to the pan along with the salt, chilli powder, black masala and coconut. Cook and stir until the excess liquid has reduced and the paste is golden, around 2–3 minutes.

Add the drained rice and stir-fry for 2 minutes. Add the vegetables, cashew nuts and 400ml water. Bring to the boil, then cover and lower the heat completely and cook undisturbed for 8–9 minutes. Taste a grain: it should be just done. Turn off the heat, remove the lid and allow any excess moisture to evaporate. Taste for seasoning and adjust if necessary and stir in the lemon juice and coriander with a fork as you fluff up the rice. It should be moist and not dry, like a pilaff.

Serves 4

3 tbsp vegetable oil
$\frac{1}{2}$ tsp mustard seeds
4 cloves
2.5cm piece of cinnamon stick
1 black cardamom pod
1 small onion, peeled and sliced
2 large cloves of garlic, peeled and chopped
3 green chillies, left whole
$\frac{1}{2}$ tsp turmeric
$\frac{3}{4}$ tsp garam masala
1 tsp fennel seeds, powdered
salt, to taste
3 medium tomatoes, chopped
200g rice, washed until the water runs
    clear and soaked while you cook
    the masala
3 tbsp fresh or frozen grated coconut

Tomato Rice

This is one of my favourite rice dishes. It is more rice, less pilaff and is normally made with southern rice, which is often thicker and shorter whilst no less delicious. However, you can use any white rice. It is a great dish that can be eaten by itself, with some yoghurt, or as an accompaniment to a lamb, chicken or vegetable dish. It is moist and moreish and full of the wonderful flavours of the south.

Heat the oil in a large non-stick saucepan. Add the whole spices and, once the mustard seeds splutter, add the onion and cook over a moderate heat until golden. Stir in the garlic and chillies, and cook over a low heat for 1 minute or until the garlic smells cooked. Add the powdered spices and salt; cook for another 20 seconds, stirring.

Add the tomatoes and turn the heat up. Cover and cook for 5–6 minutes or until the tomatoes have softened. Taste – there should be no harsh elements. Add the drained rice and stir-fry for 2 minutes. Pour in 430ml water and the coconut, give it a good stir and taste. Adjust the salt at this stage.

Bring to the boil, then cover with a tight lid, turn the heat to its lowest setting and cook for 8 minutes or until the rice is tender. Turn off the heat, remove the cover and let any excess moisture evaporate. Serve hot or warm.

4 tbsp vegetable oil
¾ tsp cumin seeds
7.5cm piece of cinnamon stick
3 cloves
3 green cardamom pods
1 bay leaf
1 small–medium onion, peeled and sliced
15g blanched almonds, halved or roughly chopped
10g raisins
200g basmati rice, rinsed until the water runs clear and soaked in water while cooking the onions
good pinch of saffron strands, soaked in 2 tbsp hot milk
2 ready-to-eat dried figs, chopped
salt and lots of freshly ground black pepper, to taste
15g walnuts or pistachios

Kashmiri Pilaff

This is a delicious pilaff that showcases the best of Kashmir's food – saffron, whole spices, nuts and dried fruit. It is slightly sweet and has lots of textures. It goes with more than just other Kashmiri dishes. In fact, the Bengalis have a sweet rice dish that is eaten with savoury food too. It looks more complicated than it actually is, but for a simpler pilaff leave out the fruit and nuts. The whole spices and onion give enough flavour to the rice by themselves. Add a little lemon juice at the end to sharpen the flavours.

Heat the oil in a large non-stick saucepan. Add the whole spices and the bay leaf and cook over a low heat for 30 seconds. Add the onion and cook until soft and golden, then add the almonds and raisins and cook for a couple of minutes.

Add the drained rice to the pan. Stir it in the spiced oil for a minute and add 400ml water, the saffron milk, figs and salt to taste. Bring to the boil and boil for a couple of minutes, then reduce the heat to its lowest setting, cover, and cook for 7–8 minutes. Taste, the grains should be cooked; if not, cover for another minute. Season and add the walnuts or pistachios. Fluff up with a fork as you stir them in. Leave for 4 minutes to allow any excess water to evaporate for a few minutes. Serve hot.

Kashmir

Kashmir was said to be paradise on Earth

and with the majestic Himalayas, the placid lakes and valleys of flowers, you can understand why. The food has been strongly influenced by the chefs brought from Samarkand in Central Asia by Emperor Timur in the fifteenth century and is mainly non-vegetarian. Kashmir is the only place where even the Hindu *pandits* (Hindus from the priestly vegetarian caste) will eat meat.

These chefs were called *wazas*. Their sole job was to cook feasts of up to 36 courses. Groups of four diners sat around and shared food from a large steel plate which held a large mound of rice, with each successive course served in four portions placed on top or to the side. Plain yoghurt and chutney were regularly eaten to cut the richness of the feast. These chefs were reluctant to teach their secrets to people outside their community and mainly handed down recipes only to their sons, but as their passion was not always passed down, many sons chose other professions. As a result, there are fewer and fewer superchefs to call upon to create the typical Kashmir banquet, now seen mainly at weddings.

The food of Kashmir is, however, a tale of two religions – the Hindu pandits and the Muslims. The main difference is that Hindus do not use the onions and garlic whilst the Muslims do, relying instead upon asafoetida and yoghurt for flavour. The cornerstones of Kashmiri food are meat, rice and yoghurt. Vegetables

such as tomatoes, leafy greens, cabbage, aubergines, lotus root and turnips are grown in floating gardens (rich soil is layered on bamboo and twigs so they always floats above the water line), which can be pulled across the water to markets. Most dishes are spiced with a local spice blend called *ver*, which is a mixture of spices, garlic and local shallots, made into a paste, kneaded into small discs and dried in the sun. Recipes for this are closely guarded and few non-Kashmiris are able to make it. However, delicious Kashmiri dishes can be made with fresh spices.

Kashmir is known as the fruit bowl of the country; they grow apples, pears, peaches, apricots, plums, strawberries and cherries. These are eaten raw when in season and dried or preserved in sugar syrup for the rest of the year. The only fruit that is cooked is the dried apricot, which is poached with spices and eaten with fresh, sweet white cheese. Desserts are rice or vermicelli-based, and often made in milk with lots of nuts and dried fruits for added texture.

Kashmiri dishes in this book include Kashmiri Lamb Kebabs (see page 31), Kashmiri Chicken (see page 80), Roganjosh (see page 116), Kashmiri Lamb cooked in Milk (see page 139), Paneer-stuffed Peppers (see page 144), Kashmiri Turnips (see page 148), Kashmiri Pilaff (see page 205) and Sweet Angel Hair Vermicelli with Orange Cream (see page 232).

Unleavened Rice Breads

Makes 10

scant ½ tsp salt
200g rice flour, plus extra for dusting
80g fresh or frozen grated coconut
handful of finely chopped shallots or onions (optional)
3 tbsp coconut milk or melted butter

These wonderful rice breads are eaten in many southern and coastal parts of India with slight variations in ingredients, thicknesses and names, but the principle is the same – bread made only with rice. This type of recipe has been influenced by the Arabs who settled in these parts of India and brought with them rich mutton curries, which are the perfect foil for these light breads. The rice or rice flour used for the softest bread is not very easy to find, so I make it with normal rice flour but the result is still delicious. Eat with southern-inspired lamb and chicken curries.

Heat 160ml water and the salt in a medium pan until it reaches a rolling boil. Add the flour and coconut all at once and stir with stick end of a wooden spoon to mix properly. Turn off the heat, cover and leave for 10 minutes. Turn out onto a work surface and knead well for 6–8 minutes. Add the onions, if using. Divide into ten balls.

Warm a tava or a flat griddle pan over a medium heat. Flatten one of the balls into a disc with your hands or a rolling pin, dip both sides in a small plate of rice flour and roll into a thin roti. The dough often cracks on the edges and many Indian cooks use a round tin lid to cut out a perfect circle. Otherwise, try to limit the cracks and fold them inwards and roll over the sides with a rolling pin again. Repeat with the remaining dough balls.

Place each bread on the pan and cook for 10 seconds or until light brown spots appear on the underside. Flip over and wait again, check underneath and flip when ready. Keep cooking, changing sides every 10–15 seconds until both sides have light brown spots. Brush with coconut milk or butter and serve, or stack one on top of the other until ready to eat, although they do get hard as they cool.

Bhakri

Makes 6 small breads

2½ tbsp ghee or vegetable oil, plus 2 tsp for cooking
100g chapatti flour, or half wholewheat flour
    and half plain flour
¾ tsp salt
good pinch of carom seeds

This delicious bread is from Gujarat. It is crisp on the outside and soft on the inside, and stays fresh for longer than many other flat breads. When I was taught the recipe, I was told that imperfections in the rolling are supposed to make it taste better, and the tiny indentations made with your fingers are reminiscent of a rustic, flat focaccia bread. It is eaten with a meal, or made in abundance for a picnic or journey and eaten with pickles and chutneys or even by itself.

Using your fingertips, mix the 2½ tablespoons of ghee into the flour until crumbly. Add the salt and carom seeds, then add 2–3 tablespoons of water. Bring together to make a dough. Knead for about 5 minutes, then leave to rest for 15–20 minutes. The dough should have a medium–hard consistency. Add more flour, if necessary, or a few drops water if too tough.

Roll the dough into a log and pinch off six equal pieces. Shape them into balls; if they crack, they need to be further worked in your hands to soften.

Heat a large frying pan over a consistent moderate–high heat. Roll three balls into circles with a diameter of 7.5cm; they should not be too thin. Place them in the pan. Cook for 20 seconds and turn them over. After another 20 seconds, turn again, this time adding ¼ teaspoon of ghee to the surface in a circular motion. Turn and repeat on the other side. Keep cooking the bread and turning, but press down on it with a round wooden implement or a cloth so the base crisps up and colours. While doing this, move the breads around the pan a little so that they are not just on one hot spot. Turn every 20 seconds. They are ready when golden on both sides, around 2–3 minutes. Repeat with the remaining dough circles.

Left: Bhakri
Right: Unleavened Rice Breads

Makes 5–6

150g chapatti flour, or half wholewheat
and half plain flour
salt (optional)

Roti

Roti, or chapatti, are basic wholewheat flat-breads that puff up when cooked and slightly crisp on the underside. It is eaten daily in Punjab, where the term for a meal is 'dal roti' – lentils and bread. There is no real skill needed, and when it comes to rolling the dough into an even circle, the old adage applies; practice makes perfect. A good knead followed by a rest will ensure the finished breads are soft. You can find chapatti flour in most large supermarkets, but you can also use equal quantities of wholewheat and plain flour. These breads can be made in advance and reheated, wrapped in foil, in a medium oven. I never put salt in my breads as they are used to mop up well-seasoned sauces, but others do – I leave it up to you. The recipe can easily be doubled up.

Sift the flour and salt, if using, into a bowl and make a well in the centre. Slowly drizzle in 100–120ml water and use your hand to draw the flour into the centre, mixing all the time. You may not need all the water as flour absorbs different amounts depending on its age and the moisture content in the air. The dough should be just slightly sticky and will firm up as you knead it.

Knead for 8–10 minutes or until the dough seems elastic and most of the joints and lines have worked themselves out. Then place in a bowl, cover with a damp tea towel and leave for 30 minutes in a slightly warm place or at room temperature in the summer.

Divide the dough into five or six equal portions and roll into golf-ball-sized balls in your hands. Cover with a tea towel. Dust your work surface and rolling pin with flour. Roll each ball into a thin circle 12.5–15cm across. The best way of doing this is to keep rolling in one direction, turning the dough a quarter of a circle to get a round shape.

Heat a tava or non-stick frying pan until quite hot. Toss the dough from one hand to the other to remove any excess flour, and place on the tava. Reduce the heat to medium and cook until small bubbles appear on the underside, about 10–20 seconds, then turn. Cook this side until the base has small dark beige spots.

The best way to puff a roti is to place it directly over an open fire using tongs – the flame of a gas hob is fine. It will puff immediately. Hold it there for 10 seconds until dark spots appear, then turn and puff the other side for a few seconds and place on a plate. Repeat with the remaining roti. If you have an electric hob, press down gently on the cooked roti in the pan – as you press one area, the rest should puff up. Then tackle the next area and the roti should puff up all over.

Keep the bread warm by wrapping in napkins or foil and keep in a low oven while you make the rest.

Raitas and Chutneys

Potato Raita

Serves 4–6

1 tsp vegetable oil
½ tsp cumin seeds
400ml natural yoghurt, stirred
250g new potatoes, boiled whole, peeled
    and cut into 1.5cm cubes
salt, to taste
handful of fresh coriander, chopped
good pinch of red chilli powder
½ tsp roasted ground cumin

This is such a lovely raita, so simple but tasty that you almost want to eat it on its own with some good naan. The soft and creamy potatoes contrast so well with the crunch of the fresh coriander and whole cumin. The red chilli and roasted cumin powders sprinkled over the top add a traditional touch to this recipe as this is how most raitas in India are garnished. I sometimes stir a spoon of sugar or, even better, tamarind chutney into this raita for a different dimension. Try it as it is and ring the changes as you please.

Heat the oil in the smallest pan you have or even in a large flameproof ladle. Add the cumin seeds and cook until fragrant and slightly darkened, then take off the heat. Stir into the yoghurt with the potatoes, salt and most of the coriander and mix well. Sprinkle a criss-cross pattern of the red chilli powder and roasted cumin powder on top. Garnish with more chopped fresh coriander and serve chilled.

Beetroot Raita

Serves 4

1 small uncooked beetroot (about 90g),
    peeled and finely diced
200ml natural yoghurt, stirred
salt, to taste
½ tsp freshly ground black pepper
1 tsp vegetable oil
1 scant tsp brown mustard seeds
1 heaped tsp sesame seeds
10 large curry leaves

I have never eaten cooked beetroot in India – my culinary experiences of them have always been raw and served sliced with a plate of other raw vegetables to provide crunch to a meal. In this state, it is so much tastier than the cooked version we are used to in the West. It is not as sweet but has a wonderful flavour and crispness that makes it an ideal raita ingredient, with the sesame seeds adding a nutty contrast. You can find raw beetroot in many grocers but if you can only lay your hands on the cooked version, it will still be a wonderful and vivid dish.

Mix together the beetroot, yoghurt, salt and pepper.

Heat the oil in a small saucepan – it helps to angle the pan so all the oil collects at the bottom. Add the mustard seeds and as they start to pop, add the sesame seeds and curry leaves. Cook until the seeds are colouring and pour into the raita. Serve it now or chill until later.

Spinach and Dill Raita

Serve 4

75g baby spinach, washed
10g dill sprigs
300ml natural yoghurt
salt, to taste
lots of freshly ground black pepper
¾ tsp roasted ground cumin

Whilst one might not associate dill with India, dill and its seeds are actually cultivated in India and exported worldwide. It can be found in many different states and has been incorporated into some of the dishes from those areas, often paired with local greens. Dill and spinach are natural partners and when used together in this dish, both flavours stand out. One of my favourite raitas, this makes a delicious and fragrant accompaniment to any Indian meal, but would also go well served with roasted or barbecued chicken or lamb or toasted pitta bread.

Place the spinach and the dill in a saucepan with a tablespoon of water and cook until soft, around 1–2 minutes. Drain and squeeze out any excess water and finely chop into shreds. Stir into the yoghurt with salt, pepper and cumin powder. Serve chilled.

Top: Spinach and Dill Raita
Centre: Beetroot Raita
Below: Potato Raita

Serves 3–4

3 tsp desiccated coconut
3 tsp chopped pistachios
3 tsp raisins, finely chopped
3 large slices of thick-cut bread
400ml natural yoghurt
1¾ tsp caster sugar, or to taste
salt, to taste
1 tsp vegetable oil
½ tsp brown mustard seeds
1–2 dried red chillies
10 curry leaves

Peshwari Bread Raita

Bread is now becoming a common substitute for a type of spongy lentil dumpling that is traditionally added to yoghurt and made into a wonderful raita. I have enhanced a simple recipe by stuffing the bread with a coconut, pistachio and raisin mixture before soaking it in the slightly sweetened and spiced yoghurt. It can be made without the stuffing and still be delicious, but it is even better with.

Mix together the coconut, pistachios and raisins.

Using a biscuit cutter (either 5cm or 7.5cm in diameter), cut out three or four circles from each slice of bread. Using a small, sharp knife, make a slit horizontally in the middle of the circles to make a deep and wide pocket. Push as much of the coconut stuffing into each pocket as possible. It doesn't matter too much if the bread breaks, as the yoghurt will hide any cracks.

Whisk together the yoghurt, sugar and salt to taste. Heat the oil in the smallest pan you have or in a large flameproof ladle. Add the mustard seeds and once they have popped for a few seconds, add the red chillies and curry leaves. Cook another few seconds and stir into the yoghurt. Taste and adjust the sugar and salt to taste.

Half an hour before serving, place half the yoghurt into a serving bowl, place the bread circles on top and cover with the remaining yoghurt. They will slowly soak up the yoghurt and soften as the yoghurt thickens.

Coriander and Mint Chutney

Serves 6 with snacks

40g fresh coriander stems and
    leaves
8g fresh mint leaves
3–4 tsp lemon juice, or to taste
salt, to taste
½–1 thin green chilli, left whole
1 small clove of garlic, peeled
3g fresh ginger, peeled
¾ tsp sugar
15 pistachio nuts (roasted is fine)

We Punjabis eat this chutney with most of our snacks and appetizers and even spread it in sandwiches. It is absolutely delicious and really simple to make. It is fresh and herby and great with grilled foods too. It is best eaten soon after it has been made as the colour will fade, but it can be kept in the fridge for a few days.

Blend all the ingredients together with 2 tablespoons of water to make a smooth purée. Taste and adjust the salt and lemon juice to taste.

Cucumber and Carrot Koshimbir

Serves 4

250g cucumber, peeled, seeds scraped out
    with a spoon and flesh finely chopped
1 medium–large carrot, peeled and chopped
    to the same size as the cucumber
175ml Greek yoghurt
3 tbsp chopped fresh coriander
½ long, thin, green chilli, seeds removed
    and finely chopped (optional)
1¼ tsp sugar, or to taste
salt, to taste
4 tbsp roasted peanuts, coarsely crushed
1 tsp vegetable oil
½ tsp black mustard seeds

Koshimbir is a salad of chopped raw vegetables, powdered peanuts and a mustard seed tarka. It is a subtle combination of sweet, salty and a little sour and spicy, adding freshness and texture to a meal. I love to mix it with yoghurt for creaminess instead of the more traditional lemon juice – if you are intolerant to yoghurt, you can add lemon juice to taste. This dish is not as loose as a raita but you can add extra yoghurt if you wish.

Mix together the cucumber, carrot, yoghurt, coriander, green chilli, sugar, salt and peanuts. Place in the fridge until ready to serve.

Heat the oil in a small saucepan and add the mustard seeds. Once they start popping, turn off the heat. When they have finished popping, stir into the vegetables. Serve cold.

Radish and Yoghurt Chutney

Serves 4

100ml Greek yoghurt
100g red radishes, grated and
    squeezed to get rid of excess
    liquid
salt, to taste
½ tsp cumin seeds, dry-roasted
4 fresh mint leaves, finely shredded
½ green chilli, deseeded and chopped
    (optional)

The recipe for this simple chutney may read more like one for a raita, but in Kashmir it is used as a chutney and mostly eaten with lamb. It works on a similar principle to that of cutting the richness of beef with horseradish, except the red radish is milder and more delicate. It goes well with any meat, from a Kashmiri kebab to barbecued lamb chops. It is also great served as a dip with naan or pitta bread.

Simply mix all the ingredients together in a bowl, then chill until ready to serve.

Top right: Radish and Yoghurt Chutney
Top left: Cucumber and Carrot Koshimbir
Below: Coriander and Mint Chutney

Ayurveda

Ayurveda is the ancient Indian 'knowledge of life'.

It is a complex and sophisticated science, incorporating all the branches of medicine, yoga, meditation and nutrition, and is basically a blueprint for how to live a healthy life with a healthy mind, body and soul. I would need an entire book to explain this philosophy in detail, but hopefully this brief overview will spur you on to learn more.

When it comes to food, we must first understand our bodies and the nature of food and only then can we make informed choices to remain in balance. It may not be exciting but it is very rewarding, as prolonged imbalances lead to illness.

According to Ayurveda, all bodies are made up of air, fire, water and matter. It is the proportions of these elements in our bodies that slot us into a body type. The three main humours or *doshas* are *vata* (air), *pitta* (fire) and *kapha* (water and matter). Once you know what your *dosha* is, and it might be two of the above, you live a life balancing it out. So *vata* (air) people should eat food that will ground them, *pitta* (fire) should eat food that is cooling on the body, and *kapha* (matter) draw the short straw when it comes to weight and need to eat dry and warm food. It is a complicated business.

To know what to eat, you have to understand the different properties of food and for that you need to ignore most things we hold as truths. Firstly, we should not judge food by calories or nutritional content, but should see our diets as a balance of the six tastes – bitter, sweet, salty, sour, pungent and astringent. We also need to take into consideration whether we should be eating food that is cooling or warming, dry or moist, and this depends both on body type and the season.

Lastly, food has subtle qualities that affect who we are and how we behave and, depending on our age, we should eat food which makes us pure of thought (*satvic*), active of body (*rajasic*) or basic and animalistic in behaviour (*tamsic*). Most of these principles are already woven into traditional Indian meals, so once we understand our body types, we can make the right choices more easily.

It is easy to dispel these beliefs as the machinations of quack doctors, but modern medicine is looking to the East to understand holistic healing and living. I have read many books on Ayurveda and find that it all makes complete, logical sense to me, and I often turn to Ayurveda to find answers to my health questions.

Bengali Tomato Chutney

Makes 100ml

1 tbsp vegetable oil
1 bay leaf
¾ tsp mustard seeds
1 dried red chilli
2 large tomatoes, chopped
¼ tsp turmeric
salt, to taste
4 tsp sugar
1 rounded tsp raisins
¾ tsp ginger paste
1 tsp white wine vinegar

Bengalis eat chutney in a different way to most other Indians, and this particular chutney is eaten after their main course and before dessert to prepare the tastebuds for something sweet. This chutney has both sweet and savoury elements, so it does seem like a natural transition from one to the other. It is thick, slightly sweet and delicious and is also great with cheese and fresh bread.

Heat the oil in a small non-stick saucepan. Add the bay leaf, mustard seeds and red chilli, and cook until the seeds start to pop. Add the tomatoes and turmeric and stir until soft. Add the remaining ingredients and 50ml water and bring to the boil, then cover and cook until it reaches a medium consistency, around 5–7 minutes.

Cool and spoon into a sterilized jar. It doesn't keep for too long, so use it within a few days.

Quick Red Chilli and Coconut Chutney

Serves 6 with snacks

4 tbsp desiccated coconut
8 tbsp coconut milk
1–1½ tsp lemon juice, or to taste
2g fresh ginger, peeled and finely grated
salt, to taste
½–1 tsp red chilli powder, or to taste
1 tsp vegetable oil
1 tsp brown mustard seeds

I love south Indian chutneys. They are hot and spicy, but the coconut provides texture and a subtle, natural sweetness. This chutney perks up any southern meal or snack and can also be served with simple grilled fish. Use soon after making or it will lose its freshness.

Stir together the desiccated coconut and milk, lemon juice, grated ginger, salt and red chilli powder until well mixed. It will be slightly sloppy but the desiccated coconut will absorb some of the water as it sits.

Heat the oil in a small pan or a large ladle and add the mustard seeds. As they pop, take off the heat. Once they stop popping, stir them into the chutney. Before you serve, have a look at the chutney – this should be a wet chutney with body. If it seems a little dry, stir in a tablespoon or two of recently boiled water. Taste and adjust the seasoning and lemon juice – it should be pleasantly tart. Serve at room temperature.

Quick Tamarind Chutney

Serves 4 with snacks

2 rounded tsp tamarind paste
35–40g jaggery, chopped up
¾ tsp cumin seeds, dry roasted until fragrant and turning brown, then ground
¼–½ tsp freshly ground black pepper
¼ tsp salt
6 fresh mint leaves, shredded (optional)

This is a really quick and easy chutney that is used in India almost as ketchup is used here – as a condiment to spice up simpler flavours. It is mainly eaten with snacks and street foods. The tartness of tamarind is balanced with the sweetness of jaggery, and the simple spices add a wonderful flavour. I often add the mint as it brings a freshness and flavour that I feel really enhances it, but this is completely optional.

Put all the ingredients in a small saucepan with 70ml water, bring to the boil and simmer for 3 minutes. Cool and store in a sterilized jar in the fridge. It keeps well for weeks.

Top: Quick Tamarind Chutney
Centre: Quick Red Chilli and Coconut Chutney
Below: Bengali Tomato Chutney

Desserts and Drinks

Serves 6

6 ripe (but not overly ripe) peaches
2 cinnamon sticks
4 whole star anise
4 slices fresh ginger
250g sugar
400ml full-fat Greek yoghurt
2–3 tsp powdered star anise (I use my
      pestle and mortar), or to taste
flaked toasted almonds, to serve

Spiced Poached Peaches with Star Anise Cream

I have always loved cooked fruits, which is definitely an English thing as fruit in India is rarely cooked. It is usually juiced or eaten raw, sometimes sprinkled with salt and pepper or spiced up until it is sweet, spicy and salty and eaten as a snack in the afternoon. This is probably due to the climate – who wants to eat warm fruits in warm weather? Peaches, especially when poached, lend themselves really well to the flavours of the sweet spices, and with a hint of ginger they are absolutely fantastic. Bengali food often ends with a sweet yoghurt dish, called *mishti doi*. The yoghurt is usually made at home and set with a caramelized sugar. I haven't set this yoghurt myself, but I have used their tradition in this light, fragrant dessert. Serve warm or at room temperature.

Cut a small cross in the skin at the bottom of each peach. Place the peaches in a large bowl and pour over boiling water to cover. Drain after 30 seconds and pour over cold water from the tap. Leave for 40 seconds, remove from the bowl and peel away the skins with the help of a sharp knife. If this hasn't worked, repeat once more.

Place the cinnamon sticks, whole star anise, fresh ginger and sugar in a large saucepan with 1.5 litres of water and bring to the boil, then cook until the sugar has dissolved. Add the peaches and cover the top of the water with a layer of greaseproof paper so that the peaches are completely submerged in the syrup. Cover with a lid and simmer gently for 10–15 minutes or until the peaches are soft when pricked with the tip of a knife (the riper the peach, the quicker it will cook). Remove the peaches to a separate dish and boil the syrup until it is reduced to about 200ml. Allow to cool. Remove the cinnamon sticks, star anise and ginger.

Stir 4–5 tablespoons of the syrup into the yoghurt along with the powdered star anise, taste and adjust the sweetness to taste. Serve the peaches scattered with flaked almonds, with the remaining syrup and a spoonful of the yoghurt.

Serves 6

1 litre full-fat milk
250g carrots, peeled and grated
3–4 tbsp sugar
good pinch of saffron strands
$\frac{1}{3}$–$\frac{1}{2}$ tsp green cardamom seeds,
    powdered
2 tbsp pistachios, chopped
2 tbsp flaked almonds, toasted
caramelized pine nuts, to serve

Carrot Kheer

I'm not convinced that words alone will persuade you that a chilled, subtly flavoured dessert of creamy, thickened milk with softened floating threads of sweet carrots contrasting with the added crunch of nuts will make the perfect Indian dessert to finish a lovely warming meal. However, most Indian desserts are based on lentils, grains, vegetables and rice and, of course, they are absolutely delicious. But in just the same way that carrot cake may seem initially unpalatable to those who have never actually tried it, the proof is in the tasting, so do try this.

Heat the milk in a wide, heavy-based saucepan, stirring and scraping the base with the spoon frequently to make sure the milk does not catch and burn. If you are standing at the cooker you can increase the heat and stir constantly, but if you are busy in the kitchen (please do not stray too far!) keep it on a low heat. Keep cooking until it reduces by about one third – this takes about 25 minutes depending on your pan and heat.

Add the carrots and continue cooking for another 15–25 minutes or until they are soft and the milk is as thick as you like it. This is a personal thing – I like it quite thin but others like it quite thick; you will need to keep up the stirring though. Stir in the sugar, saffron and cardamom powder, cook for another 2 minutes and taste for sweetness. Chilling any food dulls its sweetness, so you may need to add a little more than you would deem necessary. Cool and then place in the fridge, covered with clingfilm as milk absorbs flavours from other food in the fridge.

When ready to eat, serve in bowls sprinkled with the nuts.

Entertaining

There is a saying an old Indian saying that roughly translates to

'a guest is like god'.
I will never forget a trip to Simla with my family when I was 12. My father got chatting to the owner of a restaurant we were eating in and they exchanged stories of their lives. The next day we had a car accident and he spotted us walking into the local hospital. He asked what happened and waited for us, then took us to his home where his wife had made a meal for us. We were strangers but he treated us like family. This attitude towards receiving guests transcended all classes – both rich and poor would serve the best they could afford.

My life has been always been peppered with my parents' parties. It sometimes felt as though having a party was like putting on a theatrical production: the people, the preparations, setting the scene with flowers and a beautifully laid table and the biggest production, the meal. Once the guests arrived, all the elements had to be in place and the house came alive with laughter, colour and glamour. My entertaining style is more casual than my mother's but I can definitely see her influence – my table is always very full.

When deciding on a menu, I consider nutrition, textures and colours. It is probably easiest, in the beginning, to decide upon a meat/fish dish and then pair it with a vegetable dish or two from the same region. Of these one should have a gravy and the other will be dry and the colours should be different. Bread or rice will also depend on the provenance of the meal. A Punjabi meal will have a lentil dish too. Raita or yoghurt

is great with northern meals, but sometimes out of place with a southern coconut dish. Chutneys and pickles are also subjective, as each region has its own relationship with them. In the north, chutneys are mainly eaten with snacks and pickles generally spice up a simple meal. But in other regions, pickles are made of vegetables that are seasonal or fish/prawns as a way of preserving them and flavouring the monsoon months when few fresh ingredients are available. Some cultures eat chutney with their meals, whereas Bengalis eat a chutney after a meal; so in the absence of any proper rules, you can make your own.

The look of a dish becomes more important when feeding friends; it not only whets the appetite, but also pleases the eye. The easiest way of doing this is to use a garnish, and as long as the character of the dish is not altered, you can be as creative as you like. Some people fry mild red chilli powder in a little oil and pour it on top of their dish. In my in-laws' house they do the same with poppadoms. My family has always used fresh coriander and fried some ginger juliennes, which add texture as well as flavour. A little saffron dissolved in a teaspoon of hot milk and spooned over a simple lamb dish is also beautiful. Many people add some finely grated fluffy coconut on top as well, as a few fried curry leaves that retain their shape and colour. Nuts, raisins, pomegranate seeds and rose petals are wonderful on pilaffs or in desserts, as is silver or gold leaf.

Serves 4

3 tbsp ghee or a mixture of melted butter and vegetable oil
15g almonds, blanched and sliced lengthways (or flaked for the easy option), plus extra for serving
15g sultanas or raisins
125g very thin vermicelli, sold in Indian shops (also known as seviyan)
65g sugar

Orange cream

90ml double cream
3 tsp sugar
1¼ tsp finely grated orange rind

Sweet Angel Hair Vermicelli with Orange Cream

At least once a year, on the occasion of a large party, my mother would make traditional sweet vermicelli. She would use short, thick vermicelli, which was a sign of them being home made. As a child, I remember helping my grandmother to make them on the flat roof of her home in New Delhi. We would sit cross-legged on a rattan day bed and roll tiny pieces of the dough between our thumb and fingers, then flick these small strands onto a steel platter. They would dry in the sun and would sometimes also be dispatched to distant relatives deprived of the true ingredients of India. Sadly, the art of making fresh vermicelli has largely been forgotten and we make do with machine-made vermicelli, which lacks the texture and flavour I remember. Nonetheless, this dessert is delicious, and lighter and fresher than the traditional one. If you prefer, you can add a small scoop of ice cream instead of the orange cream served here.

Whisk together all the ingredients for the orange cream until it thickens into softish peaks. Place in the fridge until ready to use.

Heat the ghee in a medium non-stick saucepan. Add the almonds and sultanas or raisins and fry until the almonds have coloured a little. Add the vermicelli and stir-fry until they have darkened and look slightly fried and lightly roasted, around 3 minutes, stirring often.

Add the sugar and stir well for 2–3 minutes to start melting the sugar. Stir in 230ml water, cover immediately and cook over the gentlest heat for 4 minutes. Check to see if the strands are soft; if not, cover and cook for another minute or so and if necessary add another tablespoon of water. Turn off the heat and let them steam for 3–4 minutes.

Using a fork, separate the strands a little to make them fluffy (as you would with rice). Spoon into individual bowls and top with a spoon of cold orange cream. Garnish with extra nuts or grated orange rind, if you wish, and serve.

Serves 4–5

3 egg yolks
6 tbsp sugar, plus extra to sweeten
   the berries, to taste
1½ tsp cornflour
450ml whole milk
60g ground almonds (freshly ground have
   more flavour)

35g porridge oats
300g blackberries
200ml double cream
3–4 tbsp whisky (you can use any whisky,
   but I like to use single malt)
30g flaked almonds, toasted
icing sugar, for dusting

Punjabi Cranachan

Cranachan is a Scottish dessert made from porridge oats, honey, whisky and cream. The idea of this dessert came to me while I was watching a television show on the Punjabis in Scotland. In the beginning it was almost a joke – Punjabis love whisky and surely those living in Scotland would, by now, have made their own version of this alcoholic dessert. Creamy, sweet and made with a grain, it could have almost been Punjabi in origin. It is a hallmark of Indian cooks that they spice up and make their own any foreign ingredients and dishes that come their way, so it feels quite natural to do it here. In fact, I'm surprised no one has thought of it before. I have kept the basic cranachan recipe, but have made it with an almond cream, which adds a wonderful flavour and almost tastes like kheer. It can all be made in advance and assembled when ready to serve, is delicious, cooling and beautiful – all in all, a wonderful, hearty dessert.

Beat together the yolks and sugar in a bowl until creamy. Set aside.

Dissolve the cornflour in a little of the milk, then place in a saucepan with the remaining milk and ground almonds and bring to the boil over a low heat. Cook for another minute, then pour into the beaten egg yolks and sugar, whisking all the time. Pour the mixture back into the saucepan, bring back to the boil over a low heat, then cook until it thickens a little more, another 4–5 minutes. Pour into a bowl, cover with clingfilm, pressing it onto the surface to prevent a skin forming, and allow to cool.

Toast the porridge oats in a dry frying pan over a lowish heat, stirring often. This takes 4–5 minutes, but keep an eye on the oats as they can burn easily. Set aside to cool.

Purée 50g of the blackberries with enough sugar to sweeten (I use a spoon or two and sharpen with a little lemon juice). Mix in the remaining berries.

Whip the cream until soft peaks form. Stir a little of the cream into the almond cream to loosen it, then fold in the rest, along with the cooled oats and the whisky. Taste and adjust the sweetness.

Layer up the cranachan in a large glass bowl or individual glasses. Start with the almond cream, top with berries and flaked almonds and repeat. Finish with a dusting of icing sugar.

Makes 8

60g plain flour
30g icing sugar
35g ghee or melted butter
1½ tsp lime or lemon zest
1 tsp caster sugar
8 pistachios, skinned and sliced (optional)
desiccated coconut to sprinkle over
(optional)

Easy Lime Biscuits

These biscuits are so simple. They are known as sweet rotis and are often served with tea. They are traditionally cooked in a frying pan on the hob as ovens are a Western appliance; here I have given instructions for both cooking methods. The biscuits are quite short and crumbly, but as they cool they become crisp on the outside. I add lime or lemon zest to give them an extra zing, but you can leave it out or add vanilla essence or nuts or decorate them with coloured icing or sugar. The thinner you make them, the better, but even when thick they taste delicious.

Mix together the flour, icing sugar, ghee and half the zest. Work the dough until it comes together and is no longer crumbly. Pound together the caster sugar and remaining zest to make a lime-coloured sugar.

Roll the dough into 8 little balls. Work in two batches. Flatten four balls into 4cm discs in your palms, then place in a cold non-stick frying pan. Using your fingers, pat and flatten them so that they form biscuits 5–6cm in diameter, the thinner the better. Top with a sprinkling of the lime sugar and sliced nuts. Place the pan on the hob and cook over a gentle heat for 7–8 minutes. Once the base is golden, flip the biscuits carefully with a spatula. Cook this side over the lowest heat so that the tops do not colour, around 4 minutes. Place them on a plate; as they cool they will become crisp. Repeat with the second batch.

To cook in the oven, preheat the oven to 180°C/350°F/gas mark 4. Form the biscuits on a large baking sheet. Place in the oven and bake for 10 minutes or until colouring on the edges. Take out and cool the biscuits on the tray.

Serves 6–8

Coconut custard

125ml milk
125ml double cream
280ml coconut milk
5 large egg yolks
120g caster sugar
1¼ tbsp lime or lemon zest
25g cornflour
300g fresh or frozen grated coconut or
    12 tbsp desiccated coconut

Pancakes

100g plain flour
2 large eggs
1 tbsp sugar
pinch of salt
40g ghee or melted butter
8 tbsp coconut milk
200ml milk
vegetable oil, for cooking
icing sugar, for dusting

My Coconut Bebinca

Bebinca is a rich Goan dessert that takes skill, patience and practice to make. I have never tried to make it, but love the idea of a cake made from layers of thick coconut pancakes, stacked one on top of each other with nothing but ghee between them. They are then cooked in a deep pan that is placed in the oven for just long enough to cook the first layer; once cooked, a little ghee is added, another layer of batter poured in and the pan goes back in the oven. A traditional bebinca can have 16 layers, and if you burn one layer, all your efforts will be wasted. I decided to do it my way with pancakes made in my trusty pancake pan and layered with coconut custard instead of ghee. The pancakes take 30 seconds each to cook, the custard less than 10 minutes and the layering up was fun. Pancakes are a little too beige for a pretty dessert, so I often use safe food colouring and colour them. Red looks dramatic with the layers of custard, but a simple dusting of icing sugar works too.

First, make the coconut custard. Heat the milk, cream and coconut milk in a saucepan until just simmering. Meanwhile, whisk together the yolks, sugar, zest and cornflour in a bowl until smooth. Slowly pour the warm milk into the yolk mixture while whisking. Pour the whisked mixture back into the saucepan and cook over a low heat until simmering, then cook for another 2–3 minutes or until it has thickened. Stir in the coconut. Leave to cool.

For the pancakes, whisk together the flour, eggs, sugar, salt and ghee until smooth. Stir in the two milks and leave to stand for 20 minutes. Heat an 18cm pancake pan, then rub ¼ teaspoon of oil over the surface with kitchen paper. Pour about 3 scant tablespoons or 40ml of the batter into the pan and swirl so the batter covers the surface. Cook for about 20 seconds over a moderate heat, run a spatula around the edge and under and carefully turn over; cook this side for 5–10 seconds or until the underside has a few brown spots.

For the neatest finish, use an 18cm cake tin with a removable base or a cake ring. Place one pancake on the bottom, spread over 3 tablespoons of the custard. Place another pancake on top and repeat until all have been used. Unmould when ready to serve and dust with icing sugar.

If you wish to serve the pudding warm, preheat the oven to 180°C/350°F/gas mark 4. Place the tin in the oven and cook for 25 minutes. The top and base will crisp up, which is lovely but harder to slice. Dust with icing sugar to serve.

Serves 4–5

2 large or 3 medium–small Alphonso or
    Venezuelan mangoes (around
    450g flesh)
1 tsp lime or lemon juice, depending on
    how sweet the mangoes are
100g sugar
1 large egg white
2 gelatine leaves (optional, see below)
180ml double cream
handful of pistachios, chopped, to decorate

Velvety Mango Mousse

When mangoes were in season, my mother often served a large mound of jelly-like mango mousse at her parties. It was only ever made with Alphonso mangoes which, with their deep orange flesh and pure flavours, were the ideal variety for the mousse; the perfect ending to a spicy meal on those summery nights. My version is less gelatinous but I still look for that pure Alphonso flavour; the better the fruit, the better the mousse. I found some Venezuelan mangoes at my local greengrocer and, once ripe, they tasted almost Alphonso-like. This dessert takes just 10–15 minutes to make and can be made a day in advance. Gelatine is optional here, as the many vegetarian Indians will not eat it, and, when served in individual glasses, you only focus on the singing flavours of this wonderful fruit.

Cut the cheeks off the mango and remove all the other juicy flesh. Remove the skins and purée the flesh until smooth. Stir in the lime or lemon juice, if the mangoes are without acidity of their own.

Heat the sugar in a small pan with 4 tablespoons of water until dissolved, then boil to soft ball stage, around 4–5 minutes. Using a sugar thermometer is probably the easiest way of knowing if you have reached this stage (around 116–118°C), but this dish is very forgiving, so if you don't have one, don't worry.

Put the egg white in a bowl and place on a wet cloth to prevent the bowl moving. Beat the egg white until stiff, then add the hot sugar with one hand while whisking with the other (an electric whisk is best) until thick and glossy.

Place the gelatine (if using) in a small saucepan and cover with water. Allow to soften for 5 minutes. Remove the water and squeeze out any excess from the gelatine, then place it back in the pan with 2 tablespoons of water. Heat until dissolved, then stir into the mango purée and mix well.

Whip the cream until soft peaks form. Stir one-third of the cream into the mango, then spoon over the rest along with the egg whites and gently fold them both into the mango.

Spoon into a large bowl or individual glasses and leave to set in the fridge for at least a couple of hours. Top with a little freshly whipped cream and a few chopped pistachios for decoration.

244 · Desserts and Drinks

Serves 6

150g split Bengal gram (chana dal),
  washed well and soaked for as long as
  possible (I leave them overnight so
  they cook in 20 minutes)
90g sugar

¼ tsp ground cardamom
small grating of nutmeg
400g packet of filo pastry
100g butter, melted
240ml double cream
4 tbsp desiccated coconut
icing sugar, for dusting

Sweet Lentil and Coconut Millefeuille

I can see how lentils in a dessert may seem completely unappetizing, but you have to trust me here – some of India's best desserts are made with lentils and other such grains. This paste would normally be covered with Indian chapatti dough, rolled into flat breads and cooked on the hob with ghee and served hot as a dish called puran poli. It's a typical, homely dessert that would be prepared by a mother who knows she will already have the dough made for the chapattis. I was fortunate enough to be taught it by a Maharashtran. I immediately loved it and knew I had to re-invent it to fit in with my idea of dessert. So after a little experimentation, this dish was born. I absolutely love it – the soft, sweet lentil paste, crisp filo, fresh cream and desiccated coconut make it a wonderful and elegant dessert.

Boil the drained lentils in plenty of water until very soft, around 20-40 minutes. When a scum forms on the surface, skim it off. When cooked, drain the pan and purée the lentils using a hand blender, adding enough water to make a fine paste. Place back in the pan with 4½ tablespoons of the sugar, the nutmeg and cardamom. Cook for about 6–8 minutes or until the mixture comes together as a soft lump (it hardens as it cools).

Preheat the oven to 200°C/400°F/gas mark 6.

Make the filo crisps. Remove 3 sheets of pastry from the packet at a time and cover the rest with clingfilm as you work (this will prevent it drying out). Brush each sheet with a liberal amount of melted butter, sprinkle with a little of the remaining sugar and cover with another sheet of pastry. Brush again with butter and sprinkle with sugar and place the remaining sheet on top. Brush with butter. Using a 7.5cm pastry cutter, cut out 6 circles. Repeat twice, using 9 sheets of pastry in total (this takes less time than it first appears).

Place the 18 circles on a baking sheet lined with greaseproof paper. If you want the crisps to have a flat finish, top with another sheet of the paper and another baking sheet. I like the top crisps to have more character and colour, so I leave at least 6 unpressed. Bake for 5–6 minutes or until golden. Remove from the oven and leave to cool.

Whip the cream in a bowl to form soft peaks.

Place the lentil paste in a piping bag (or in a sandwich bag and snip off the end). Pipe the paste in a circle on top of 12 pastry crisps – the paste should completely cover the base and be about 7.5mm thick. Sprinkle with ½ teaspoon of desiccated coconut each. Spread or pipe a heaped teaspoon of the whipped cream on top of the coconut.

Make up your stacks by placing one bountiful disc on top of the other, cream side up and top with a plain pastry crisp. You can serve them immediately or place in the fridge until ready to serve. Bring back to room temperature, dust liberally with icing sugar and serve.

Serves 2

300g blackberries
200ml natural yoghurt
½ tsp lemon juice
1½ –2½ tbsp sugar, depending on
    the sweetness of the berries
ice cubes and mint leaves, to serve

Blackberry Lassi

This is such a vibrant lassi – it has the most beautiful purple colour and is fresh with the flavours of the sweet-sour blackberries. It is perfect for the summer with some ice cubes but also makes a fantastic, healthy, between-meals drink which is lighter and better than your mid-afternoon coffee or tea break.

Purée together the berries, yoghurt, lemon juice and most of the sugar with 140ml water. Sweeten to taste. Pour through a sieve into glasses to remove the seeds. Serve chilled over ice cubes, with a mint leaf on top for colour and freshness.

Glossary

This glossary explains some of the more unusual ingredients or terms used in some of the recipes. As well as the more familiar English translations for ingredients, I've also given the Indian names that you may come across in Indian stores. If you have any difficulty buying some of the ingredients, on page 256 there are some useful mail-order websites.

Spices

Asafoetida (heeng)

This is a really pungent powder that helps digestion, and as such is added to many dishes that can be difficult to digest. Use the smallest pinch as it is very strong. If you don't have any, leave it out – it won't affect the dish too much.

Black/brown cardamom pod (badi elaichi)

These large woody pods look as though they are well past their sell-by date, but they have a wonderful and strong flavour when cooked. They are an important element in garam masala and pilaffs.

Black peppercorns (kali mirch)

Little needs to be said here, except that the taste and aroma of freshly ground peppercorns is far superior to store-bought powder.

Black salt

A mined rock salt that is actually pink-grey in colour. Its defining feature is that it has a natural sulphuric flavour. It is used sparingly in tamarind chutney and is one of the main ingredients in chaat masala.

Brown mustard seeds (rai)

These brown seeds are used a lot in India. They are to the south what cumin is to the north. They are also a key element in pickle making. When added to hot oil, the seeds will splutter, so it is a good idea to have a cover handy to stop them popping out of the pan. Once cooked, they become almost nutty. When ground into a powder, they provide a tart note to dishes and when ground into a paste they are the very essence of mustard.

Carom seeds/bishops weed (ajwain)

A small dark green seed that is reminiscent of thyme. It is quite strong so you only ever need to use a little. We often use it with fish and in some Indian breads. It is also an instantaneous cure for a stomach ache. Take half a teaspoonful with a pinch of salt and drink with hot water.

Cassia/cinnamon

The bark of the cassia tree is very similar to cinnamon except that it is coarser and the flavour is less delicate. It is interchangeable with cinnamon and is often ground into a powder and sold as cinnamon. We often cook with it in India as it is cheaper than its cousin and has a good flavour but not so much sweetness.

Chaat masala

A blend of spices that few Indians make at home. It is spicy and tart and Indians sprinkle it over many cooked foods, and even drinks, for a kick of flavour.

Cinnamon

See cassia.

Cloves (laung)

A strong spice that is most commonly used in garam masala. The natural oil in this is great for a toothache – bite down on the clove where it hurts and hold it there for as long as possible.

Coriander seeds and powder (sabut dhaniya)

Coriander seeds come from the flowers of the coriander plant. They are mild and aromatic and are abundantly used. They have a subtle flavour but once you know what they taste like, you can always identify their presence. I often drink coriander-seed tea after meals as it helps digestion and is cooling on the body. The seeds, when powdered or ground, are used as a base for many masalas and it is probably the most used spice in my kitchen. Good-quality store-bought powder will be mossy green rather than brown.

Cumin seeds (jira)

This familiar spice is earthy when cooked in oil and nutty when dry roasted. It is an important spice in our cooking and adds a lovely rounded flavour. Great for digestion when made into a light warm tea.

Curry leaves (kari patta)
These leaves are truly fragrant. They add a taste of the south to any dish they are added to.

Dried mango powder (amchur)
This ingredient is actually made from dried raw mangoes. It is tangy and we often sprinkle it on to cooked tandoori foods or fried potatoes instead of lemon juice or vinegar. It doesn't need cooking.

Fennel seeds/aniseeds (saunf)
A sweet, liquorish-like spice. They are often seen in the cuisine of Kashmir but also in the south. They are good for the stomach, and cooling and great for breast-feeding when infused in hot water. Also a natural breath freshener – chew on a few after a meal.

Fenugreek seeds and leaves
These small, hard seeds need to be added sparingly as they have a strong flavour and aroma often reminiscent of curry houses. The fresh leaves are an acquired taste as they have a bitter quality. We believe that you need a balance of tastes in the body so bitterness is necessary, but eating these leaves is never medicine – they are delicious when cooked with tomatoes or potatoes to balance the bitterness. One variety of fenugreek leaves is dried and the flavour is more savoury than bitter. These are added to a dish at the end for a new flavour dimension. The dried version is called kastoori methi and is much easier to find than the fresh variety as they are not dependent on seasons.

Garam masala
This famous blend is at its purest composed of the strong flavours of cloves, black cardamom, cinnamon and green cardamom. We add bay leaves, mace and black peppercorn to this. Many milder brands will add coriander and cumin seeds. This powder can be added towards the end of cooking for a real punch of aroma or closer to the beginning for a more rounded, subtle taste. See also pages 12–13 for spice blend recipes.

Green cardamom pod (chotti elaichi)
This is one of my favourite spices. It has a soft but powerful aroma and is used in sweet and savoury dishes and is essential in spicy tea. The seeds can be ground to make green cardamom powder.

Mace (javitri)
A wonderful flavour that goes very well with meat and chicken.

Nigella seeds (kalonji)
These delicate black seeds have a peppery flavour but without the bite.

Panch phoran
This is a Bengali spice blend that consists of fenugreek, mustard, fennel, cumin and nigella seeds all mixed together in equal proportions. It is available ready mixed in Indian supermarkets.

Red chilli powder (lal mirch)
This is usually very hot and adds great colour to a dish but not much flavour.

Saffron (kesa)
Saffron is the dried stamen of the crocus flower. It is very expensive but a little goes a long way and it keeps well in the fridge. It has a lovely, musky flavour that works in both savoury and sweet dishes. Try to find long stamens.

Turmeric powder (haldi)
This vibrant powder is essential in Indian cooking. It is prized for its colour and its fantastic medicinal properties.

White poppy seeds (khus khus)
These are the same as the familiar dark poppy seeds but without the black husk. The skinless seeds have a smoother character.

Lentils

Bengal gram (channa dal)
The whole bean is similar to the chickpea but smaller and with a dark brown skin. Once skinned and split, the bean becomes a wonderful, earthy, yellow lentil.

Brown lentils (whole masoor dal)
These are actually small, slightly plump beans, and if you look closely, you will see the evidence of the pink/red lentil under their skins. They take a long time to cook but are absolutely delicious and very healthy, easy to digest. They are one of my favourites.

Red lentils (split masoor dal)
These beautiful lentils have a wonderful salmon red colour that unfortunately changes to yellow as you cook them. I sometimes add a little paprika powder to maintain the salmon tones. They are really easy to digest and have a slight sweetness to them. Their character makes them go from soft to mush very quickly, but this is not always bad as the flavours are still there.

Split and skinned black gram (urad dal)
This small, delicate lentil is used a lot in south Indian food for texture, as it is sautéed to a nutty crunch without being pre-boiled.

Split and skinned mung bean (dhuli mung ki dal)
This small, pale yellow lentil is one of the easiest to digest and has a subtle, buttery flavour. At home, this is the lentil we eat most.

Split yellow pigeon pea lentil (toovar/arhar dal)
This lentil is often cooked until it completely breaks down to a smooth paste and is then spiced before being served. Wash well before cooking as it is usually coated in a film of oil to help preserve it.

Flours

Chapatti flour
A blend of whole-wheat and plain flour that is used to make our most common flatbreads. It can be found in Indian stores as well as many of the larger supermarkets. Substitute with equal quantities of plain and whole-wheat flour.

Gram flour (besan)
A key ingredient in Indian cookery and made from powdered Bengal gram. Northern Indians use it to make batters, to bind marinades in tandoori foods, to flavour vegetables and also to make simple wheat-free breads. It has more protein than wheat. It can now be found in large supermarkets.

Rice flour
In India rice flour would be made by soaking the grains, drying them in the sun and then grinding them to a fine powder. This is used to add crispness to fried foods, to make dumplings in the south, to thicken curries and in the north to make a ground rice pudding. I love this delicate and fragrant flour and use it as a thickener instead of cornflour.

Others

Buttermilk
A by-product of the butter-making process. It may seem like a tangy version of skimmed milk but, once flavoured, it is absolutely delicious and easier to digest than milk or yoghurt.

Coconut (fresh, frozen, desiccated)
Coconut is available as a whole nut, chopped into large pieces (from some supermarkets), desiccated and now, my new discovery – finely grated and frozen (from Asian stores). It is just the best invention. I buy it, break it up into large chunks and then put it back into the freezer for ready-grated coconut, defrosted in minutes, and no elbow grease required.

Coconut cream is simply made from the grated flesh ground with a cup of water and left to drip through a sieve into a bowl. More water is then added to the residue and the process repeated to produce coconut milk. However, you get really good-quality milk in cans now so few people will take the trouble to make it fresh. Store the milk in the fridge, but it will last only 3–4 days before turning rancid.

Fruit salts
Eno fruit salts are an ingredient that used to be used in earlier times to relieve indigestion, but they are also a fantastic leavening agent. Available in most pharmacies, as well as Indian stores.

Ghee (clarified butter)

Prized for its medicinal qualities in the East. It has a strong aroma and burns at a higher temperature than butter.

Jaggery (gur)

This is a completely unrefined sugar and probably the healthiest sugar around. It is made by boiling the natural sap from the date palm until it is hard and sets in a block. It is full of minerals and has a host of healthy properties. Buy the darkest you can find as it is less watery and has a more defined flavour.

Masala

A masala simply means spice – this could be a single spice or a blend of spices or it could mean the base of the gravy that has been spiced. When thinking about a cooked masala, all you have to remember is that each stage must be done properly, in accordance with the recipe. Impatience will lead to a flavourless or raw dish.

Paneer

This traditional Indian cheese is made without rennet or bacterial culture (see page 13). It is similar to fresh farmer's cheese and it looks like solid ricotta. I think it is fabulous and it is an important source of protein for Indian vegetarians.

Pilaff

A term used for any spiced and seasoned rice dish. It can be simple or contain any number of added ingredients.

Raita

A term used for yoghurt once it has had ingredients added to it. You can add cooked or raw, crunchy vegetables or even fruit to it. A wonderful summery dish that is great with barbecues as well as full-on Indian meals.

Tamarind (imli)

The tamarind tree bears wonderful pods of fruit, which are thick, fibrous and full of large seeds. But once softened and strained, the tamarind paste is a wonderful, tangy ingredient. It has a fruity, sour flavour and is used prolifically in the south, often to balance the sweetness of the coconut in their curries. Tamarind blocks and paste are both available. A block of tamarind is simply dried tamarind in a very raw state. This has to be rehydrated in water and then sieved to remove the fibres and stones. The resulting liquid is used to add sourness to a dish. Tamarind paste is a concentrated version of this liquid. Different brands have different densities and levels of tartness so always add to taste.

Tarka

A tarka is simply spiced oil. It often refers to oil that is spiced and flavoured and added to a cooked dish, so that the flavours are fresher and more vibrant than if you had cooked all the spices in the main dish.

Cooking equipment

Karahi

A karahi is a wok-like, non-stick pan with a rounded base. This allows the food to move easily in the pan without sticking to the edge and burning. Once you begin to use these pans, you'll never want to go back to straight-sided saucepans!

Tandoori cooking

A tandoor is a barrel-shaped clay oven and is so popular that tandoori food is now eaten all over the world. The temperature in a tandoor can reach 500°F and this type of oven gives dishes a barbecue-like flavour by searing them on the outside.

Tava

We cook most of our flat breads in this shallow, concave cast-iron pan. The pan holds the heat well and bread cooks quickly and evenly. If you don't have one, a non-stick frying pan also gets the job done.

Index